JUDGING DEMOCRACY

Judging Democracy

Christopher Manfredi and Mark Rush

broadview press

LIBRARY AND ARCHIVES CANADA CATALOGUING IN PUBLICATION

Manfredi, Christopher P. (Christopher Philip), 1959–
    Judging democracy / Christopher Manfredi and Mark Rush.

Includes bibliographical references and index.
ISBN 978-1-55111-702-7

    1. Election law—Canada—Cases. 2. Election law—United States—Cases.
3. Constitutional law—Canada—Cases. 4. Constitutional law—United
States—Cases. 5. Democracy—Canada. 6. Democracy—United States.
I. Rush, Mark, 1961– II. Title.

KE4622.M36 2008   342.71'07   C2007-907543-6
KF4483.E4M36 2008

BROADVIEW PRESS is an independent, international publishing house, incorporated in 1985. Broadview believes in shared ownership, both with its employees and with the general public; since the year 2000 Broadview shares have traded publicly on the Toronto Venture Exchange under the symbol BDP.

We welcome comments and suggestions regarding any aspect of our publications—please feel free to contact us at the addresses above or at broadview@broadviewpress.com / www.broadviewpress.com.

NORTH AMERICA
Post Office Box 1243,
Peterborough, Ontario,
Canada K9J 7H5

2215 Kenmore Ave.,
Buffalo, New York, USA 14207
TEL: (705) 743-8990
FAX: (705) 743-8353

customerservice@broadviewpress.com

UK, IRELAND, & CONTINENTAL EUROPE
NBN International, Estover Road, Plymouth,
UK PL6 7PY
TEL: 44 (0) 1752 202300
FAX: 44 (0) 1752 202330
enquiries@nbninternational.com

AUSTRALIA & NEW ZEALAND
UNIREPS University of New South Wales
Sydney, NSW 2052 Australia
TEL: 61 2 96640999
FAX: 61 2 96645420
infopress@unsw.edu.au

Broadview Press acknowledges the financial support of the Government of Canada through the Book Publishing Industry Development Program (BPIDP) for our publishing activities.

Designed and typeset by Em Dash Design

 This book is printed on paper containing 100% post-consumer fibre.

Printed in Canada

To Paula and Sophie.
To Flor, William and Alex.

Contents

Acknowledgements

We gratefully acknowledge the support of the Government of Canada's Canadian Studies Grant Program administered through the Canadian Embassy in Washington, DC. and the Social Sciences and Humanities Research Council of Canada

Introduction

If there is one constant theme in the scholarly literature concerning American and Canadian constitutional law, it is that the two nations are quite different.[1] According to this view, the US Bill of Rights and the Canadian Charter of Rights and Freedoms, are based on fundamentally different visions of rights. The American document and constitutional tradition promote individual rights and place substantive restrictions on the capacity of government to legislate for the common good. By contrast, the Canadian Charter is much less individualistic in both its text and interpretation.

We have written this book in part to refute this analysis. While scholars can easily point to cases in which the Canadian and American supreme courts arrived at opposite conclusions, we argue that they have overstated the implications of these differences. This is especially true with regard to case law concerning the democratic process. Distinctions that the Canadian Supreme Court seemed to establish between itself and the US Supreme Court early in the Charter era have withered away as both courts have struggled with the intricacies of democratic rights and the intractable complexity of laws governing the democratic process. The result has been a remarkable convergence in thinking between the two supreme courts.

This convergence was most clearly manifested in the 2003–04 term. In December 2003 and June 2004, the United States and Canadian supreme courts rejected challenges to their respective nations' campaign spending laws. In *McConnell v. Federal Election Commission* and *Harper v. Canada*, respectively, the two courts used essentially the same reasoning to sustain the constitutionality of campaign spending restrictions.[2] Majorities on both courts deferred to the desire of Parliament and Congress to constrain campaign spending and political speech in order to promote equality and foster public confidence in the political process. The dissents in both cases asserted that the challenged laws restricted free speech and threatened to render the political process less competitive. Even more striking is that the common dissents were voiced by justices who could not have seemed more different: Chief Justice Beverly McLachlin of the Canadian Court and Associate Justice Antonin Scalia of the American Court. We suggest that when two such justices find common ground, something important is at work and merits investigation.

We originally intended simply to refute scholarly assertions of difference by using election case law to demonstrate the commonality of the two courts' thinking. Insofar as neither constitution clearly or explicitly defines the scope of the franchise, the two supreme courts have had to fashion such definitions themselves. This process of development has occurred as part of what Peter Hogg and Allison Bushell describe as an ongoing dialogue with the national and provincial or state legislatures as these elected branches have sought to regulate the electoral process—ostensibly, to make it fairer.[3]

However, we found that this convergence was accompanied by a simultaneous development of a suspicion within both courts that their respective legislatures might put partisan divisions aside and engage in cartel-like behaviour to buffer themselves from electoral competition.[4] This skepticism has placed the courts of both nations in the same awkward position. On the one hand, in order to adjudicate challenges to election laws, the courts must fashion clear definitions of the rights at stake. On the other, jurists and scholars in both nations have also acknowledged that, in the absence of clearly defined constitutional rights, courts ought to exercise restraint and defer to legislative attempts to define and balance democratic rights. Insofar as there are many aspects of democratic theory, a court cannot justify imposing one particular democratic vision precisely because the people (and their elected representatives) might prefer a different yet equally justifiable vision of democracy. To impose one democratic vision upon the political process would not only interfere with the legislative process but also risk debilitating the polity's capacity to deliberate and develop its capacity for self-government.[5]

Finally, scholars and some members of both courts recognize that, if the courts are too deferential, they risk enabling the legislatures to behave in a cartel-like manner and, literally, lock themselves into power at the expense of or despite the polity's desire to hold elected officials accountable or remove them from office.[6] This conundrum was clearly evident in *Harper* and *McConnell*. The two courts divided into two groups: one that trusted, and therefore deferred to the legislature's capacity to regulate the democratic process, and one that did not.

Accordingly, our analysis of the convergence in the two courts' thinking demonstrates two common aspects of the struggle with democracy. First, both courts have engaged in a common struggle to define democratic rights in the absence of textual guidance from their respective constitutions. This in turn has led to a second common struggle to define and refine their relationship with the legislature in light of the skepticism of legislative motive that has arisen from the courts' struggle to define democratic rights. Both courts agree—generally—that the franchise embodies a right to cast a vote that is *meaningful* in an electoral process characterized by real competition among electoral options.

Both courts have also experienced difficulty in applying these broad notions to particular election law controversies. As a result, the academy has been divided in its analysis of the two courts' case law. While some scholars and jurists have said that the courts have adhered to clear theoretical visions of democracy,[7] others have said that the courts either have no theoretical vision[8] or, at best, a muddled one.[9]

The absence of a coherent constitutional vision of democracy or a clear theoretical approach to it in either court is neither a cause for criticism nor alarm. Both courts have husbanded their visions of "meaningful" democracy over time. While some court members have tried to adhere to a particular theory of politics, we agree with Daniel Lowenstein that neither court abides by a particular theory of politics (at least not yet) and that this is a good thing.

An attempt to subscribe to one democratic vision would hamper the courts' ability to engage in a dialogue with the legislature. In fact, we find that if one difference still endures between the two supreme courts in this area of the law, it lies in the Canadian Court's propensity to impose a particular theoretical vision of democracy. This puts an end to the dialogue with the legislature and truncates the process of deliberation that is vital to democratic development. This poses an important challenge to Canadian democracy and we discuss it in our closing chapter.

Structure of the Book

In the following chapter we discuss the assertions from early in the Charter era by Patrick Monahan, in particular, about the differences between Canada and the United States. We then present three case studies in which we compare the two nations' jurisprudence with regard to criminal disenfranchisement, redistribution and "rep by pop," and restrictions on campaign spending and political speech. The case studies provide the evidence on which we base our refutation of assertions of difference between Canadian and American election case law. We then conclude with a discussion of the skepticism of legislative motive that both courts now manifest, as well as the implications of the Canadian Court's activism for the constitutional dialogue in Canada.

Notes

1   See, e.g., Patrick Monahan, *Politics and the Constitution: The Charter, Federalism and the Supreme Court of Canada* (Toronto: Carswell, 1987); Mary Ann Glendon, *Rights Talk: The Impoverishment of Political Discourse* (New York: Free Press, 1991); C. Lynn Smith, "Adding a Third Dimension: The Canadian Approach to Constitutional Equality Guarantees," *Law and Contemporary Problems* 55 (Winter 1992): 211–34. See also McLachlin's speeches as cited in the following chapters.

2   *McConnell v. Federal Election Commission*, 540 U.S. 93 (2003) and *Harper v. Canada*, [2004] 1 S.C.R. 827.

3   See Peter W. Hogg and Allison A. Bushell, "The Charter Dialogue between Courts and Legislatures," *Osgoode Hall Law Journal* 35 (1997): 75–107.

4   See, e.g., Peter Mair, "Party Organizations: From Civil Society to the State," in *How Parties Organize: Change and Adaptation in Party Organizations in Western Democracies*, ed. Richard S. Katz and Peter Mair (London: Sage Publications, 1994).

5   See Alexander M. Bickel, *The Least Dangerous Branch: The Supreme Court at the Bar of Politics* (Indianapolis: Bobbs-Merrill, 1962); John Hart Ely, *Democracy and Distrust* (Cambridge: Harvard University Press, 1980); Monahan, *Politics and the Constitution*; Stephen G. Breyer, *Active Liberty: Interpreting Our Democratic Constitution* (New York: Alfred A. Knopf, 2005).

6   See Samuel Issacharoff and Richard Pildes, "Politics as Markets: Partisan Lockups of the Democratic Process," *Stanford Law Review* 50 (February 1998): 643–717; Samuel Issacharoff, "Gerrymandering and Political Cartels," *Harvard Law Review* 116 (December 2002): 593–648.

7   See Colin Feasby, "*Libman v. Quebec (A.G.)* and the Administration of the Process of Democracy under the Charter: The Emerging Egalitarian Model," *McGill L.J.* 44 (1999): 5–39; Colin Feasby, "The Supreme Court of Canada's Political Theory and the Constitutionality of the Political Finance Regime," in *Party Funding and*

Campaign Spending in International Perspective, ed. Samuel Issacharoff and K.D. Ewing (Oxford: Hart Publishing, 2006); and Heather MacIvor, "The Charter of Rights and Party Politics: The Impact of the Supreme Court Ruling in *Figueroa v. Canada (Attorney General)*," Montreal: Institute for Research on Public Policy, *Choices* 10 (2004): 2–26.

8   See Daniel H. Lowenstein, "The Supreme Court Has No Theory of Politics—and Be Thankful for Small Favors," in *The U.S. Supreme Court and the Electoral Process*, ed. David K. Ryden (Washington, DC: Georgetown University Press, 2000).

9   Compare, for example, Jamie Cameron, "Governance and Anarchy in the s. 2(b) Jurisprudence: A Comment on *Vancouver Sun* and *Harper v. Canada*," *National Journal of Constitutional Law* 17 (2005): 71–103; and Christopher D. Bredt and Markus F. Kremer, "Section 3 of the *Charter*: Democratic Rights at the Supreme Court of Canada," *National Journal of Constitutional Law* 17 (2005): 19–70.

chapter one

Differences That Matter?
Canadian Misreading of American Constitutionalism

The extent to which the American Constitution has influenced Canadian constitutional development remains a subject of debate and controversy among Canadian scholars. At first glance, the argument in favour of significant differences between Canadian and American rights jurisprudence finds support in the text of the Charter itself. Although it resembles the US Bill of Rights in many ways, the Charter is in other important respects a politically indigenous document. It protects some distinctively Canadian rights, such as general language rights and minority language education rights. It also contains an explicit limitations clause (section 1), as well as a potentially more effective check on judicial power (section 33) than the provisions listed in Article III of the US Constitution (which sets out the powers, jurisdiction, and structure of the US federal judiciary). Moreover, the Charter does not expressly protect private property rights, nor does it contain anything like the "takings" clause of the Fifth Amendment to the US Constitution.[1]

Despite these differences, early commentators recognized the potentially positive impact of American civil rights jurisprudence on Charter adjudication.[2] Indeed, the evolution of the Charter suggests a conscious effort by its drafters to allow for the incorporation of some elements of US civil rights jurisprudence into Charter adjudication, while avoiding the more problematic details of the US experience. On the positive side, the Charter's architects removed the reference to "a parliamentary system of government" from section 1 in order to ensure that Canadian courts would not completely ignore American constitutional jurisprudence when adjudicating Charter issues.[3] At the same time, however, provincial concerns about the interpretation given to the phrase "due process" by American courts led to its replacement with "principles of fundamental justice" in section 7 of the Charter.[4]

In practice, the attitude of Canadian commentators toward the US experience has ranged from enthusiastic praise for judicial enforcement of constitutional rights in the United States,[5] to warnings about misusing or misunderstanding American constitutional theory and experience.[6] Initial judicial attitudes toward the American experience were similarly mixed. In the Supreme Court's first Charter decision, *Law Society of Upper Canada v. Skapinker* (1984), Justice Willard Estey remarked that "it is of more than passing interest to those concerned with these new developments in Canada to study the experience of the United States courts."[7] Striking a more cautious note, Justice Antonio Lamer argued in the *B.C. Motor Vehicle Reference* (1985) that the use of American jurisprudence must be tempered by judicial recognition of the "truly fundamental structural differences between the two Constitutions."[8] Similarly, Justice Gerald La Forest suggested in *Rahey v. The Queen* (1987) that "American jurisprudence ... must be viewed as a tool, not as a master."[9] In 1988, Chief Justice Brian Dickson synthesized these attitudes when he wrote in *Simmons v. The Queen* that, while Canadian courts "must ... be wary of adopting American interpretations where they do not accord with the interpretive framework of our Constitution, the American courts have the benefit of 200 years of experience in constitutional interpretation. This wealth of experience may offer guidance to the judiciary in this country."[10]

Scholarly criticisms of US constitutionalism manifest a conscious desire to emphasize that the Canadian jurisprudential road is not the same one taken by the United States. Therefore, the Charter established a unique Canadian approach to questions of rights in general and the electoral process in particular.[11] American commentators like Mary Ann Glendon have noted, for example, that the Canadian Charter "diverges in both letter and spirit from its American counterpart in important respects.... [it] has avoided hard-edged, American style proclamations of individual rights." As well, she says that the framers of the Charter, in contrast to their American counterparts, emphasized the need to balance individual and community interests.[12]

Scholars of election law emphasize the "marked contrast" of the Canadian experience to that of the United States with respect to judicial oversight of laws concerning the electoral process. As John Courtney said, the differences are "a product of the greater acceptance in Canada than in the United States of the responsibility of government to establish electoral practices that are non-partisan and whose effect will be as widely inclusive of the citizenry as possible."[13]

Other recent work on Canadian and American jurisprudence concerning campaign spending limitations makes similar attempts to distinguish the two nations. Colin Feasby began his analysis of campaign spending law by stating that "[o]pponents of the wholesale importation of U.S. political finance jurisprudence into the U.K. and Canada welcomed the recent decisions of the European Court of Human Rights ... and the Supreme Court of Canada in *Bowman v. United Kingdom* and *Libman v. Quebec*, respectively."[14] Janet Hiebert concludes a commentary on the Canadian Supreme Court's decision in *Harper v. Canada* with the following statement: "Until the majority Supreme Court ruling in *Harper* Canadian judges had become alarmingly close to the position taken by the US Supreme Court ruling in *Buckley v. Valeo*, which held the notion of fairness in elections as foreign to the constitutional values that underlie the political community."[15] The desire to demonstrate some distance between Canada and the United States is palpable.

We believe that the differences between the American and Canadian regard for rights in general, and electoral rights in particular, are overstated. In this chapter, we draw upon Patrick Monahan's *Politics and the Constitution* to discuss some key Canadian misperceptions of the differences between the United States and Canada. We demonstrate that the American Supreme Court has been much less individualistic than Monahan suggested regarding rights in general and property rights in particular.

As well, we argue that the American Court has also been more willing than Canadian critics have admitted to engage the elected branches in a dialogue about constitutional development. Our observation stems in part from our refutation of arguments about the American preoccupation with property rights, as well as a reliance on writings by Associate Justice Stephen Breyer about American constitutional development and the role of the Supreme Court.

In addition, we demonstrate that the Canadian Supreme Court is not as disposed to engage in a dialogue with the federal and provincial legislatures as some Canadian scholars suggest. In several notable instances the Court has shed the deferential attitude described by Monahan and asserted its primacy in constitutional interpretation. More important, we demonstrate in the ensuing chapters that the evolution of the Supreme Court's election law decisions actually undermines the basis for deferring to (and therefore engaging in a dialogue with) the elected branches.

Monahan and the American Founding: A Straw Figure?

In *Politics and the Constitution*, Patrick Monahan offered an interpretation of the spirit of democracy that informs the Charter. He distinguished Canadian constitutionalism from that of the United States, asserting that while there are "many similarities between American and Canadian legal culture," the distinctions between them are so telling that the grounds for contrast outnumber those for comparison.[16]

"Canadian politics," said Monahan, "has always placed particular emphasis on the value of community, in contrast to the overriding individualism of the American experience."[17] While the establishment of individual rights in the Charter did seem to administer a "potent dose of individualism" to the Canadian body politic and move Canada somewhat toward the individualism of the United States, Monahan maintained that this individualism is tempered by the Tory (or communitarian) traditions of Canada.[18] Accordingly, rights claims in Canada could not be regarded in the same manner as they are in the United States: "American writing on judicial review does not really provide adequate answers to the difficult interpretive issues which arise under the *Charter*. The *Charter* is a uniquely Canadian document. The key to unlocking its secrets does not lie in an alien culture, but in the Canadian political tradition itself."[19]

The principal distinction between Canadian and American political traditions lies in how the two nations balance individual rights claims and corresponding assertions of community interests and rights. Monahan explained that the two nations differ in the extent to which they regard individual rights claims as "fundamental" values that can trump the public interest. On the one hand, both nations embody a scholarly tradition that is guarded in its support for judicial review of legislation and the corresponding judicial protection of individual rights claims at the expense of the majority's right to govern.[20] Yet, as Monahan noted, this shared skepticism of judicial review is overshadowed by important differences in the two nations' constitutional traditions.

> [D]emocratic objections to the judiciary enforcing a set of "fundamental values" are as persuasive in the Canadian as in the American context. But, there are a series of additional, equally compelling difficulties with any attempt to import this form of judicial review into the Canadian setting.

These difficulties arise from a fundamental tension between the assumption underlying the "fundamental values" position and the distinctive quality of the Canadian political tradition.

In the Canadian setting, the community's collective interest or right is as "fundamental" as that of the individual dissenter. Therefore, regardless of the fundamentality with which an individual asserts his or her rights claim, the Canadian constitutional vision does not regard such assertions as trumps. Instead, individual and community rights claims must be balanced. Monahan continued:

> The assumptions underlying a "fundamental values" version of judicial review are profoundly individualistic. The language of "trump rights" encourages the belief that communities are nothing more than aggregations of private interests. The rightholder is defined by his separation from and opposition to the community as opposed to his membership in it. This is exemplified by the assertion that the state remains neutral on questions of the good life or of what gives value to life.[21]

The Canadian belief that the state is more than simply a "neutral" political actor reinforces a difference in the two nations' jurisprudence. Monahan argued that the Canadian state is expected to lead and promote particular visions of the good life—that is, the "public interest." This conception of the good life may come at the expense of the unfettered exercise of individual liberty or rights, even if they are enumerated in the Charter. Thus, wrote Monahan, Canada promotes a communal vision of rights that contrasts markedly with the "impoverished" vision of community that inheres in the United States. The American vision of rights is suspicious of any attempt by "the state" to assert a particular vision of the "public interest."

This suspicion of the state and the desire to force it to remain neutral is clear in James Madison's discussion of the evils of faction in *Federalist* 10.[22] Madison viewed politics as a struggle among competing egoistic interests that would use the state apparatus to advance those interests despite or at the expense of other competing or antithetical interests. In this vision of politics there is no truly "public" interest. Instead, there is the interest of the majority that just happens to control the government at a particular moment. Accordingly, from this perspective, it would make sense, as Monahan noted, to cast individual rights as a means of separating oneself from and defending oneself against "the community," because one is not really a member of the community if he or she is not a member of the governing majority.[23]

The Charter's enumeration of rights, Monahan emphasized, embodies "fundamental Canadian values as opposed to fundamental American, British or European ones."[24] Therefore, the Charter must be interpreted in a communitarian light—not in terms of the "profoundly individualistic philosophies of Ronald Dworkin and other American 'fundamental rights' theorists."[25]

Dworkin's vision of rights was, indeed, a totemic statement of individualism. As he noted in *Taking Rights Seriously*, "If someone has a right to something, then it is wrong for the government to deny it to him even though it would be in the general interest to do so." This is, Dworkin continued, "the distinctive concept of a right against the State which is the heart, for example, of constitutional theory in the United States."[26] As we discuss below, however, while this may be one way to envision the "heart" of American constitutional theory, the American Court has not adhered to this vision of individual rights.

Monahan observed that the Charter is grounded on two values: the promotion of democracy and the promotion of community. Democracy is more than just popular rule. It entails, he said, "a broadening of the opportunities for and the scope of collective deliberation and debate in a political community; it means identifying and reducing the barriers to effective and equal participation in the process by all citizens; it means ensuring that there are no arbitrary and permanent boundaries around the scope of political debate."[27]

This forms a key basis for distinguishing the American and Canadian constitutional traditions. Whereas the Canadian Charter is aimed at collectively enhancing and protecting the integrity of Canadian democracy, Monahan maintained that the American Constitution is designed to protect individual rights at the expense of the collective good. It is therefore "simply implausible to regard the provisions of the American constitution as being directed exclusively towards the enhancement of democratic values."[28] The unyielding judicial protection of individual rights in the United States debilitates the democratic process (in the words of one author)[29] and prevents the people's elected representatives from legislating in the public interest if doing so encumbers individual rights claims. The "democratic" conception of judicial review that animates the Charter is therefore much broader than the individualistic vision that informs the American Constitution: "the drafters of the Canadian *Charter* embraced those elements of the American constitution designed to protect the democratic process, while largely excluding provisions aimed at guaranteeing particular substantive goods or values deemed fundamental."[30]

Monahan explained that these "substantive goods or values" are individual rights and their protection: "far from promoting democracy, the [American Constitution] seems preoccupied with drawing boundaries around the political process and preventing unruly majorities from interfering with established rights, particularly property rights."[31] This focus on individual rights will always suggest that there is a "right answer" to any constitutional conflict involving rights: When in doubt, the Court should protect the individual right from encroachments by a majority.

Monahan argued that the Canadian constitutional tradition is designed to promote—not debilitate—the people's capacity for self-government. It is based on the principle that "judicial review should be conducted in the name of democracy, rather than as a means of guaranteeing or requiring 'right answers' from the political process."[32] This "democratic" conception of judicial review diminishes the fundamentality (or, at least, the prima facie validity) of individual rights claims in favour of protecting collective values. For Monahan, then, judicial review should be

> a mechanism to protect existing opportunities for democratic debate and dialogue as well as to open new avenues for such debate. The democratic conception stands in contrast to various "justice-based" theories, designed to circumscribe and bypass the political process. By inviting judges to test the substantive fairness of political outcomes against some independent normative standard, justice-based theories limit the opportunities for popular participation and control. Rather than encouraging individuals to debate and define the conditions of their communal life, conflict is arbitrated by deferring to an elite judiciary.[33]

Thus, a democratic conception of judicial review calls for judicial restraint so that the elected branches of the government can engage the polity in a substantive discussion of issues and policy. Resorting to the courts for the resolution of political conflict simply truncates this deliberative process and, ultimately, harms the democracy by diminishing (or atrophying) its collective capacity to engage in and manage political conflict (including rights claims).

Monahan said that a principal basis for the contrast between Canadian and American constitutionalism was the latter's inclusion of a property right in its Bill of Rights. To be sure, there is no disputing the importance of the property right in American revolutionary thinking. Even Alexis de Tocqueville was compelled to comment on the importance of the property right in the American political psyche: "In no country in the world is the love of property more active and more anxious than in the United States; nowhere does the majority display less inclination for those principles which threaten to alter, in whatever manner, the laws of property."[34]

However, a preoccupation with the property right does not translate into a willingness to sacrifice the common good in the manner Monahan described. We therefore believe that Monahan miscast its role in American constitutional thought. While he argued that the property right clearly demonstrated America's commitment to individualism at the expense of community, we demonstrate that the US Court has consistently supported legislative restraints on the property right in the public interest. As well, recent writing by Justice Stephen Breyer of the US Court demonstrates that there is a strong current of American constitutional thought that is sympathetic (if not quite similar) to the vision that Monahan attributed to Canada. We now turn to discuss this misreading of American constitutionalism.

The Property Right: Proof of American Individualism?

The American founders were concerned with the threats posed to property by debtor relief laws passed by state legislatures in the 1780s. The ease with which property could be seized by the legislatures kindled the framers' desire to build protections of property and contract into the new constitution, while also constructing the federal system in a manner designed to make it quite difficult for the government to act quickly or in a cohesive manner: "A particular concern for Federalist thought at the time was to protect property against seizure by a "tyrannical" majority; the ambition was to minimize the threat implicit in popular political power rather than to facilitate political participation or democratic empowerment."[35]

In contrast to the individualistic property right, Monahan cited the more positive conceptions of Charter rights (such as language rights), which presume a symbiotic relationship between the state and the rights-bearing individual. Whereas Monahan's rendering of the eighteenth-century property right casts the individual in a defensive position vis-à-vis a rapacious state, the language right is, by definition, dependent on the state for its exercise and assumes that there is a complementary community right that must be protected as well. One cannot exercise language rights without the existence of a community with whom to communicate. Therefore, again, the state must foster and protect the community that defends and gives meaning to the right.[36] In contrast, one can exercise the right to speak at the expense of, or in opposition to, a community.

The individualistic view of the American Founding is not uncommon. But this same aspect of the Founding can be viewed in radically different ways. In her seminal work, *The Concept of Representation*, Hanna Pitkin affirms Monahan's observation. In the American (Madisonian) vision of constitutional government, "the danger [posed by governmental power] is action and the safeguard is stalemate."[37] In seeking to constrain the power of the government, the American framers saw government not acting in the public interest but, having been taken over by a particular factional interest, using the governmental institutions to pursue that discrete agenda under the guise of "the popular will" or the "public good."

Thus, Monahan might look back at the American Founding and regard the encumbrance of property via debtor relief laws simply as good public policy. However, at the time, the Federalist framers saw the debtor relief laws as disputes between at least two groups of people who had competing visions of the best way to manage the economy. There was no clear public or collective interest. Instead, there were many interests at stake and there was no way to resolve this conflict in a positive-sum manner. Instead, the conflict had to be managed. Thus, as Pitkin notes, Madison regarded representative government as a place where social conflict "can be controlled by balancing and stalemating."[38]

This vision of political conflict and constitutional government is hardly grounded in the unyielding protection of individual (in this case, property) rights as Monahan suggested. While some scholars suggest that the Federalists were more concerned with containing the threats of republican government than they were with nurturing its promise,[39] others suggest that the protection of individual rights—especially the property right—was grounded precisely in the desire to promote republican government.[40]

First, one might note that the Federalists themselves cast the property and contract right in instrumental terms. Private property and contracts were not simply substantive values to be protected at the expense of a greater common good. Instead, their protection ensured that the economy would grow, and that investors would risk their wealth for public and private gain. As Madison noted in *Federalist* 44:

Our own experience has taught us, that additional fences against these dangers ought not to be omitted. Very properly, therefore, have the convention added this constitutional bulwark in favor of personal security and private rights. The sober people of America are weary of the fluctuating policy which has directed the public councils. They have seen with regret and indignation that sudden changes and legislative interferences, in cases affecting personal rights, become jobs in the hands of enterprising and influential speculators, and snares to the more industrious and less informed part of the community. They have seen too, that one legislative interference is but the first link of a long chain of repetitions, every subsequent interference being naturally produced by the effects of the preceding. They very rightly infer, therefore, that some thorough reform is wanting, which will banish speculations on public measures, inspire a general prudence and industry, and give a regular course to the business of society.[41]

This is hardly the stuff of unfettered protection of the propertied minority. Instead, Madison's reasoning here indicates that property rights were vital, at the time, to the public good that comes with the establishment of a stable economy and democracy.

In this regard, the American founders anticipated the concerns of those scholars today who assert the importance and necessity of establishing a fair, predictable, and rational system of property rights for the growth of developing countries. Stable economies form a key part of the foundation of stable democracies. Thus, while the Federalist language may sometimes appear to be highly individualistic, the thrust of the *Federalist* papers can certainly be cast in terms of nation-building, as well as the protection of individual rights.

Furthermore, recent writing by United States Supreme Court Justice Stephen Breyer indicates that the protection of individual rights was, in fact, driven by a desire to promote (not contain) the republican aspects of American politics. We turn now to discuss Breyer's competing interpretation of the American founders' vision of rights. We will then demonstrate how the history of American property rights jurisprudence conforms to his more collective, less individualistic vision of the American constitutional milieu.

Justice Breyer's Recasting of American Individualism[42]

Breyer argues that rights have "active" (i.e., "ancient") and "negative" (i.e., "modern") components and interpretations. Faithful interpretation of the constitutional text does not prohibit a judge from seeking to balance these different components of rights in a manner that he or she deems most favourable for society. Insofar as Breyer believes that the Constitution embodies a commitment to promoting the people's liberty to engage in an "active and constant participation in collective power,"[43] he argues that judges should strike the balance between ancient and modern liberty in a manner that has the most favourable consequences for the democratic process.

In a statement that echoes Monahan's description of Canadian constitutionalism, Breyer asserts that the American Constitution promotes ancient active liberty, that is "the people's constitutional right to an active and constant participation in collective power," because "greater judicial emphasis upon active liberty will help to bring about better law." Better law, he argues, "is law that enables the community to find practical solutions to important social problems through fair, open, and collective deliberation."[44]

The text of the American Constitution casts liberty and rights in a negative manner by articulating what cannot be done by Congress or to the people. However, Breyer asserts, these negative grants of rights must be regarded as part of a constitutional milieu that promotes a positive collective vision of political participation. The Madisonian separation of powers, the establishment of a federal division of powers, the staggering of electoral terms, and so forth were all, according to Breyer, designed to complement the negative rights protections by ensuring that individuals so protected from government would be able to participate effectively in the political life of the nation. This view, he says, regards

> the framers as seeking to create a form of government in which all citizens share the government's authority, participating in the creation of public policy. It understands the Constitution's structural complexity as responding to certain practical needs, for delegation, for non-destructive (and hopefully sound) public policies, and for protection of basic negative freedoms.[45]

Negative freedom from government would be of little value if it resulted in the unfettered exercise of liberties by the few at the expense of the many. Therefore, Breyer sees the Madisonian system as a network designed to control the more powerful elements in society by making it difficult for them to threaten the rights of minorities or individuals either by taking over the government or by throwing their weight around disproportionately in civil society. It cannot be that Madison sought to unleash on civil society the factions he sought to control in *Federalist* 10.

The Role of the Judiciary in Breyer's Vision

The establishment of a better democracy by promoting active ancient liberty imposes a duty on the courts to behave modestly—if not deferentially—when striking down legislation. There is a twofold basis for this. First, the many more heads present in the legislature are likely to be more circumspect than the considerably fewer heads present on any court.[46] Accordingly, promotion of the Constitution's democratic objective entails deferring to the collective wisdom of legislatures.

Second, unless the legislature has perpetrated an egregious violation of rights, such deference in and of itself promotes the Constitution's democratic objective by allowing the process of representative government to play out. In this respect, Monahan celebrated the educational aspects of political delibera- tion,[47] and Breyer echoes him. As Monahan wrote: "Democratic politics is not guaranteed to produce right answers.... A choice for democracy means that the community has a right to be wrong."[48] And Breyer agrees that courts should not truncate political debate or impose a "correct" answer on a political dispute: "[E]ven if a judge knows what the just result should be, that judge is not to substitute even his juster will for that of the people."[49] Instead, the people must develop political experience and obtain moral education and stimulus that comes from correcting their own political errors.[50]

This deference to the legislature and tolerance for the deliberative incre- mentalism that will naturally characterize a healthy democracy promotes better law by fostering the process of self-government. Thus, Breyer does not simply make a politically conservative call for judicial restraint. Instead, he argues his theory

> finds in the Constitution's democratic objective not simply restraint on judicial power or an ancient counterpart of more modern protection, but also a source of judicial authority and an interpretive aid to more effective protection of ancient and modern liberty alike.... increased emphasis on that objective by judges when they interpret a legal text will yield better law—law that helps a community of individuals democratically find practi- cal solutions to contemporary social problems.[51]

Breyer accordingly argues that the US Constitution regards individual rights in much less fundamental terms (and therefore more permissibly the object of legislative compromise) than Monahan suggested. Breyer envisions a proc- ess of constitutional development akin to a dialogue about the scope and definition of rights between the courts and the elected branches, such as that described by Canadian scholars like Peter Hogg.[52] Judicial review is therefore less about the protection of fundamental values than it is about addressing competing concerns about how to balance numerous rights claims. As he says: "[A] judge's agreement or disagreement about the wisdom of a law has nothing to do with the right of the majority to embody their opinions in law." A judge should not impose the "just result" on the deliberative process.[53]

Constitutional Dialogues

Breyer's rejection of the notion that courts can or should impose a "just result" on the process of political deliberation echoes statements made a decade earlier by Justice Frank Iacobucci of the Canadian Court. In 1998, Iacobucci chastised those who suggested that Canadian courts are "wrongfully usurping the role of the legislatures" for having misunderstood "what took place and what was intended when our country adopted the Charter."[54] Rather than posing a danger to "democratic values," as these critics and commentators alleged, Justice Iacobucci argued that the Charter promotes a "dialogue between and accountability of each of the branches" that has "the effect of enhancing the democratic process, not denying it."[55] In making this assertion, Justice Iacobucci gave the Court's imprimatur to the idea that the Charter's structure provides an ingenious solution to the problem of judicial supremacy. According to this "dialogue metaphor," or theory of "dialogic constitutionalism," the presence of a reasonable limits clause (section 1) and legislative override (section 33) ensure that courts cannot use "rights talk" to have the last word on public policy.

The dialogue metaphor to which Justice Iacobucci alluded had its origins in an article by Peter Hogg and Allison Bushell.[56] Although the Hogg/Bushell article is as well known as any in recent Canadian legal scholarship, it is nevertheless useful to summarize its argument. The article's purpose is to confront critiques of the Charter that are "based on an objection to the legitimacy of judicial review in a democratic society."[57] The Hogg/Bushell strategy was to pursue an "intriguing idea ... raised in the literature ... [but] ... left largely unexplored. That is the notion that judicial review is part of a 'dialogue' between the judges and legislatures."[58] Although there are some instances where dialogue is precluded,[59] Hogg and Bushell argue that structural features of the Charter ensure that the "normal situation" is one in which "the judicial decision to strike down a law can be reversed, modified or avoided by the ordinary legislative process."[60]

The structural features to which Hogg and Bushell refer, and which Iacobucci affirmed, are fourfold.[61] First, section 33 gives legislatures the ultimate power of legislative override. Second, section 1 allows legislatures to implement and defend alternative means of achieving important objectives following judicial nullification. Third, some rights are internally qualified and therefore do not constitute an absolute prohibition on certain actions. Finally, the Charter contemplates a variety of remedial measures short of nullification. Taken as a whole, these features of the Charter mean that it "can act as a catalyst for a two-way exchange between the judiciary and the legislature on the topic of human rights and freedoms, but it rarely raises an absolute barrier to the wishes of the democratic institutions."[62] To Hogg and Bushell, the theory and practice of dialogue meant "that the critique of the *Charter* based on democratic legitimacy cannot be sustained."[63]

Hogg and Bushell themselves recognized that the idea of dialogue in constitutional interpretation was not particularly novel.[64] So why did their particular version of the argument attract Justice Iacobucci's attention? The answer to this question lies in their empirical analysis of "legislative sequels," which they defined operationally as "some action by the competent legislative body" following judicial nullification.[65] Examining 65 cases in which a court struck down legislation on Charter grounds, they found that 80 per cent of those decisions had evoked a legislative response.[66] In addition, the exercise of judicial review encouraged legislatures to engage in "Charter-speak" by incorporating the language of Charter review ("pressing and substantial objectives"; "reasonable limit") into statutory preambles.[67] Finally, they found dialogue in judicial deference, as legislatures identified flaws in statutes that required correction in the process of defending them, even where courts did not detect a constitutional violation.[68] In some ways, Hogg and Bushell suggested that Canadian courts had fulfilled the Charter's promise of transforming "rights-talk" into "democratic conversation."[69] Where others had discussed dialogue as an abstract possibility, they claimed it had become a concrete reality.

Kent Roach took up the dialogue metaphor a few years later in *The Supreme Court on Trial*.[70] Like Hogg and Bushell, Roach was responding to charges that the Canadian Supreme Court had become dangerously active under the Charter. In his view, the Court's critics were mired in a dead-end American debate rendered moot by the Charter's structure. According to Roach, the Charter is a product of a "creative compromise that combined the virtues of both legislative and judicial activism."[71] Again, like Hogg and Bushell, Roach emphasized the importance of sections 1 and 33 to this compromise. To quote him at length:

The requirement in section 1 of the *Charter* that limits on rights be prescribed by law followed common law traditions of demanding clear statements for the infringements of rights. It enhances democracy by requiring legislatures to articulate, and presumably to debate, the limits they place on rights. Section 33 similarly requires legislatures expressly to declare that legislation will operate notwithstanding certain *Charter* rights. It also requires the legislature to revisit the matter in calmer times when the override expires after five years. Section 1 and section 33 remain distinctive features of the *Charter* that would be unthinkable to most Americans, who believe that rights are absolute and that courts should have the last say on rights.[72]

These distinctive features of the Charter's approach to judicial enforcement of rights, Roach continued, distinguish it from that of the American Constitution[73] and have made it highly attractive to other legal systems.[74]

The key to dialogic constitutionalism, then, is that, "[u]nder the Charter and modern bills of rights, legislatures can still respond to court decisions by limiting or overriding the rights the Court has proclaimed."[75] Roach's preferred theory of democratic dialogue is one in which courts and legislatures perform distinct but complementary roles. The role of courts is to "bring to the attention of legislatures and society important values, such as fairness and minority rights, that politicians and bureaucrats would often prefer to ignore," while the role of legislatures is to expand and refine the terms of the debate and to make clear "why rights have to be limited in particular contexts," or even overridden in exceptional circumstances.[76] The result is "a process in which all of us in a democracy can struggle together for the right answers, without relying on the monologues and concentrated power produced by either judicial or legislative supremacy."[77]

What does dialogue mean in practice? As alluded to above, Hogg and Bushell offered two very different definitions of "dialogue" in their original article. First, they suggested that "[w]here a judicial decision is open to legislative *reversal, modification, or avoidance*, then it is meaningful to regard the relationship between the Court and the competent legislative body as a dialogue" (emphasis added). Where this condition is met, they continued, "any concern about the legitimacy of judicial review is greatly diminished."[78] A few pages later, in setting out their empirical test for dialogue, they indicated that "the 'dialogue' to which this article refers consists of those cases in which a judicial decision striking down a law on *Charter* grounds is followed by *some action* by the competent legislative body" (emphasis added).[79] This second definition of dialogue is much broader than the first and increases the likelihood of finding the phenomenon with which they are concerned. In our view, the greater precision of the first definition makes it more useful analytically. The practical question, then, is what it means for a legislature to "reverse, modify, or avoid" a Charter nullification of legislation.

Legislative reversal of a Charter decision is the most aggressive response to judicial nullification. It entails a legislature's rejecting outright a court's basic constitutional holding that there is a conflict between the impugned action and the Charter. The principal device for reversal is section 33, which stipulates that legislatures can declare that statutes shall operate "notwithstanding" a range of Charter-protected rights for a renewable period of five years. However, for reasons explored elsewhere, legislative reversal in this sense is rare indeed.[80] By contrast, modifying judicial nullification involves legislative acceptance of a court's basic constitutional holding but takes advantage of the opportunity provided by the usual practice in Charter adjudication of combining judicial affirmation of legislative objectives with constitutional concerns about the means selected to pursue those objectives.

Of the three possible dialogic responses available to legislatures, avoidance is the most difficult to define. In one sense, it can refer to the obvious point that legislatures can always avoid judicial nullification by persuading courts that legislation does not violate the Charter. As it turns out, legislatures are actually quite successful at "litigative" dialogue, prevailing in about two out of every three Charter cases decided by the Supreme Court.[81] The decision to appeal a lower court loss, and the process of defending legislation in increasingly senior appellate courts should thus be understood as an important aspect of judicial-legislative dialogue; indeed, it is the most direct form of dialogue. But are there techniques of avoidance available to legislatures when the Supreme Court finally strikes down legislation? One obvious form of avoidance is simply to ignore the decision. Legislatures might also avoid Charter decisions by withdrawing from the relevant policy area. However legislatures approach avoidance, it can only be considered dialogic if it leaves the predecision policy status quo unchanged or produces a new status quo that differs significantly from the one approved by the Court. Legislative inaction that results in the implementation of the Court's preferred policy position by default does not really satisfy the requirements of dialogue.

To many observers of the Charter, especially outside of Canada, the dialogue metaphor describes a mechanism through which Canada has successfully implemented a constitutionally entrenched, judicially enforceable bill of rights that simultaneously avoids the democratic threat posed by judicial supremacy. Yet, there may be reasons to be skeptical about the success of this mechanism. In particular, the Charter's structure—especially section 1—may not be as robust a remedy for judicial supremacy as the dialogue theorists suggest.

Section 1 of the Charter, which provides that the rights and freedoms set out in the document are "subject only to such reasonable limits prescribed by law as can be demonstrably justified in a free and democratic society," recognizes that constitutionally guaranteed rights cannot be absolute in a functioning society. In this respect, section 1 is similar to the "giving reasons" requirement that animates judicial review of administrative decision-making in the United States and other jurisdictions. Under this requirement, rule-making discretion is mildly constrained by the obligation to "inform the citizens of what [decision-makers] are doing and why."[82] In fact, much of the Canadian Court's interpretation of section 1 is consistent with this.

Of the section's four distinct elements—"reasonable limits," "prescribed by law," "demonstrably justified," and "free and democratic society"—two have raised few interpretive questions.[83] The Court has interpreted "prescribed by law" to mean that any limitation of Charter rights must be expressly contained in legislation, regulations, or (under certain circumstances) court orders. Consequently, actions by government officials (e.g., law enforcement officers) that infringe Charter rights are not salvageable under section 1 unless they are expressly authorized by a law or regulation. The Court has defined "demonstrably justified" to mean that governments bear the burden of proving that the Charter infringements they seek to uphold are justifiable. In this respect, limitations on rights must be systematic and purposeful rather than ad hoc and random.

If this were all that section 1 entailed, then it would only provide the basis for procedural review of government action. However, as Martin Shapiro argues, it is very difficult to prevent the "giving reasons" requirement from becoming a substantive standard of review. The reason for this "inevitable and peculiarly easy" shift, according to Shapiro, is that the requirement to give reasons forces decision-makers "to give a fairly full account of the factual basis for [their] decisions, making it far easier for judges to second-guess those decisions."[84] It is relatively easy, Shapiro argues, for courts to move from "did not give reasons," to "did not give *good* reasons," to "did not give *good enough* reasons." Ultimately, the distinction between "good enough reasons" and "good enough policy" breaks down. "Indeed," Shapiro concludes this point, "in rejecting various offered reasons, a court can usually signal what substantive policy it would accept."[85] In fact, one can see this shift in the Court's interpretation of the third and fourth elements of section 1.

At one level, the term "free and democratic society" has been interpreted to mean that legislation limiting Charter rights should be compared to similar measures operating in other free and democratic societies. At another level, Chief Justice Dickson suggested in 1986 that this term means that Charter limitations should be measured against the "values and principles essential to a free and democratic society," which include "respect for the inherent dignity of the human person, commitment to social justice and equality, accommodation of a wide variety of beliefs, respect for cultural and group identity, and faith in social and political institutions which enhance the participation of individuals and groups in society."[86] Limitations on rights, in other words, must serve a set of substantive principles. The obvious difficulty is that these "values and principles" are both indeterminate and often internally irreconcilable. For example, reasonable people can disagree about the practical consequences of respecting the inherent dignity of the human person, just as this value can conflict with respect for cultural and group identity. The result is that the term "free and democratic society" licenses judicial discretion rather than constrains it.

The same can be said for "reasonable limits." The Court offered its first definitive interpretation of this term in *R. v. Oakes* (1986).[87] The *Oakes* test, as it came to be known, contains two elements. First, the government seeking to defend the limit in question must show that its legislative objective relates "to concerns that are pressing and substantial in a free and democratic society." Second, the limit itself must be proportionate to the legislative objective, which courts determine according to a three-pronged proportionality test. To pass the first prong of this test, the limit must be rationally connected to the legislative objective. Next, the government must show that, by impairing the relevant right or freedom as little as possible, the limit in question represents the least restrictive means of achieving this objective. Finally, it must be clear that the collective benefits of the limitation outweigh its individual costs. Although superficially procedural, proportionality and minimal impairment analyses represent strong forms of substantive review. This is because they imply that a court can envision a better law than the one under review in the sense that the court's alternative would achieve legislative goals at less cost to competing rights claims.[88]

This problem is apparent in the Court's attempt to vary the application of the *Oakes* test according to the type and intended beneficiaries of a public policy. The Court began to articulate this variation on the *Oakes* test in

Edwards Books and Art v. The Queen (1986), where it cautioned against the adoption of "rigid and inflexible standards" of review in circumstances where legislatures have limited rights in order to promote the interests of otherwise disadvantaged groups.[89] Three years later, in *A.-G. Quebec v. Irwin Toy* (1989), Chief Justice Dickson elaborated on this principle by stating his belief that the Court "must be cautious to ensure that [the Charter] does not simply become an instrument of better situated individuals to roll back legislation which has as its object the improvement of the condition of less advantaged persons." For the first time in *Irwin Toy*, the Court drew an explicit distinction between policies that mediate the claims of competing groups and those where government "is best characterized as the singular antagonist of an individual."[90] For policies of the first type, Dickson suggested, the Court should be circumspect in assessing legislative objectives and means. By contrast, the second type of policy frees the Court to exercise its review function more aggressively. However, as we argue below, this distinction is both untenable and nonbinding.

The most obvious example of the second policy type, according to Dickson, is an infringement on legal rights. In this context

> the state, on behalf of the whole community, typically will assert its responsibility for prosecuting crime whereas the individual will assert the paramountcy of principles of fundamental justice. There might not be any further competing claims among different groups. In such circumstances, and indeed whenever the government's purpose relates to maintaining the authority and impartiality of the judicial system, the courts can assess with some certainty whether the "least drastic means" for achieving the purpose has been chosen, especially given their accumulated experience in dealing with such questions.[91]

The justification for judicial activism, or at least a lesser degree of deference, in the legal rights field rests, therefore, on a general distinction between socio-economic policy and criminal justice policy, and on a distinction within criminal justice policy itself between criminal *law* and *procedure*.

At first glance, the Court's approach to these distinctions appears both consistent and unproblematic. Where legislatures have sought to balance competing claims in complex areas of socio-economic policy, or where the criminal law is alleged to violate rights that are not essential to the criminal process itself, the Court exercises restraint. Only in procedural matters, where courts have an important responsibility to protect individuals from state coercion, and also possess a unique expertise, is judicial activism unequivocally legitimate.

As a general constraint on judicial activism, however, this policy distinction is extremely unsatisfactory. Even where the state is engaged in balancing competing claims in complex areas of socio-economic policy, the outcome will produce winners and losers. In some limited cases, the losers will be no worse off than if the government had not made a particular policy choice, and their Charter claim may simply stem from an assertion that a different choice might have made them better off. In most other cases, however, once the government strikes a balance in favour of one interest over another it becomes the adversary of the losing interest. This is particularly true where either provincial regulatory statutes or federal criminal law is the vehicle for striking that balance.

Edwards Books and Art, Irwin Toy, R. v. Keegstra (1990),[92] and *R. v. Butler* (1992)[93] provide an excellent illustration of the difficulty. Although these cases involved government attempts to protect vulnerable groups, they also involved enforcement through provincial penal law or criminal prosecution. Consequently, the Court's deference to legislative policy choices in these cases cannot be explained by the absence of an adversarial relationship between the individual and the state. In the final analysis, the distinction between socio-economic balancing and adversarial infringement of individual interests is not sufficiently tangible to provide the foundation for a principled guide to judicial action.

Indeed, the Court has been inconsistent in following the implications of its apparent general rule of judicial deference in socio-economic policy cases. For example, in *RJR Macdonald v. A.-G. Canada* (1995), it stated that "to carry judicial deference to the point of accepting Parliament's view simply on the basis that the problem is serious and the solution difficult, would be to diminish the role of the courts in the constitutional process and to weaken the structure of rights upon which our constitution and our nation is founded."[94] In this case, the result was a strict rather than deferential application of the *Oakes* test in a policy area where deference might have been the guiding principle. In sum, the Court is unwilling to follow even self-imposed limits on its judicial review function, and its control over the interpretation and application of section 1 allows it to expand and contract those limits to suit its immediate policy preferences.

Dialogues, Deference, And Democracy: The Development of the Property Right in American Constitutional History

In the same way that the Canadian Court is not as disposed to engage in dialogic constitutional interpretation as Hogg and Bushell suggest, the American Court resembles the deferential or dialogic body that Justice Stephen Breyer describes more than it does the unyielding defender of individualism that Monahan and others have suggested.[95]

Breyer's assertion that the vision of the American framers was more complex and inclusive than Monahan suggests is supported by the development of American constitutional law concerning the property right. A host of decisions from the Supreme Court dating back to the early nineteenth century indicates that, contrary to Monahan's characterization, the Court did not promote the protection of individual property rights at the expense of the public good. In fact, the opposite is true.

A powerful early example of this occurred in *Charles River Bridge v. Warren* (1837).[96] In 1785, the Massachusetts legislature incorporated the Charles River Bridge Company to construct a bridge and collect tolls. In 1828, the legislature granted the Warren Bridge Company the right to build a free bridge nearby. The new bridge deprived the old one of traffic and tolls. The Charles River Bridge Company filed suit, claiming the legislature had defaulted on its initial contract, which it claimed granted a monopoly to the Charles River Bridge Company.

A strict individual rights reading of the contract clause in the American Constitution might have resolved the case in favour of the Charles River Bridge company.[97] The Supreme Court instead ruled against Charles River, asserting that the contract right did not exist at the expense of the common good.

The object and end of all government is to promote the happiness and prosperity of the community by which it is established; and it can never be assumed, that the government intended to diminish its powers of accomplishing the end for which it was created ...

The whole community ... have a right to require that the power of promoting their comfort and convenience, and of advancing the public prosperity ... shall not be considered to have been surrendered or diminished by the state unless it shall appear by plain words that it was intended ...

> While the rights of private property are sacredly guarded, we must not forget that the community also has rights, and that the happiness and well being of every citizen depends on their faithful preservation.[98]

Even in dissent, Justice Joseph Story cast the property right and its protection in instrumental terms:

> I can conceive of no surer plan to arrest all public improvements, founded on private capital and enterprise than to make the outlay of that capital uncertain and questionable both as to security and as to productiveness. No man will hazard his capital in any enterprise, in which, if there be a loss it must be borne exclusively by himself; and if there be success, he has not the slightest security of enjoying the rewards of that success for a single moment.[99]

Thus, as far back as the early nineteenth century, the United States Supreme Court subjugated the contract clause and the property rights associated with it to the common weal.

Later in the nineteenth century, the Court reasserted the presumption that the common weal outweighed that of discrete interests in property in *Munn v. Illinois* (1876).[100] In this case, the Court upheld state regulations of grain elevators despite protests by their owners that this regulation constituted a taking of property without due process.

> Looking then to the common law, from whence came the right which the constitution protects, we find that when private property is affected with a public interest, it ceases to be *juris privati* only ... When therefore one devotes his property to a use in which the public has an interest, he, in effect grants to the public an interest in that use and must submit to be controlled by the public for the common good.[101]

Thus, while property was unquestionably an important individual right, the Court did not regard it as an impregnable barrier against state intervention in the public interest. Property owners could not have their cake and eat it too. If they used their private property to engage the forces of the public marketplace, they could not cry foul if their property rights were somehow encumbered by market forces or the rules governing the marketplace.

This was made especially clear in *Home Building and Loan v. Blaisdell* (1934),[102] where the Court upheld the Minnesota Moratorium Law of 1933.

Minnesota had placed a two-year moratorium on mortgage foreclosures in order to stabilize the depression-ridden economy. Mortgagors protested because their investments had effectively been seized for two years longer than the terms to which they had agreed in their mortgage contracts. Accordingly, the Moratorium Law was challenged both as a violation of the contracts clause in Article I of the Constitution, as well as the property right in the Fifth and Fourteenth Amendments. Here again, the Court asserted that all contracts presuppose the existence and preservation of a state police power.

> Not only are existing laws read into contracts in order to fix obligations as between the parties, but the reservation of essential attributes of sovereign power is also read into contracts as a postulate of legal order. The policy of protecting contracts against impairment presupposes the maintenance of a government by virtue of which contractual relations are worthwhile.[103]

Thus, the circumstances of the Depression required states to alter contracts and property rights in order to stave off the possibility of economic disaster even before the Court surrendered to Franklin Roosevelt's court-packing plan and reversed its opposition to New Deal economic policies.

In *Hawaii Housing Authority v. Midkiff* (1984), the Court sustained Hawaii's reallocation of private land.[104] In Oahu, for example, 22 private landowners controlled more than 72 per cent of the private real estate. The state legislature acknowledged that this concentration of landownership was detrimental to the state's economy and the general welfare of its citizens. The Land Reform Act of 1967 allowed the state to condemn residential real estate. The Hawaii Housing Authority would then seize the condemned property, compensate the original landowners, and then resell the land in smaller parcels to the people who had been renting it.

The Fifth and Fourteenth Amendments allow the taking of private property for a public use. In *Midkiff*, the Court expanded the definition of "public use" to include the transfer of land from one owner to another if the state deemed it necessary to promote a greater public interest. This deference to the elected branches' desire to balance individual and collective rights was manifested in an extremely controversial manner most recently in *Kelo v. City of New London* (2005),[105] where a closely divided Court upheld New London, Connecticut's use of the eminent domain power to seize private homes and then sell the land on which they were located to a private developer (Pfizer) who planned to build a research park and thereby promote economic revitalization of the city.

The Court refused to "second-guess the city's considered judgments about the efficacy of its development plan" and similarly, declined to "second-guess the City's determinations as to what lands it needs to acquire in order to effectuate" the economic redevelopment plan.

> It is not for the courts to oversee the choice of the boundary line nor to sit in review on the size of a particular project area. Once the question of the public purpose has been decided, the amount and character of land to be taken for the project and the need for a particular tract to complete the integrated plan rests in the discretion of the legislative branch.[106]

The dissenting justices lamented the majority's abandonment of the property right to the whims of a legislature's definition of a public purpose. This same spirit animated countless academic and journalistic criticisms of the decision, which argued that the Court had essentially sacrificed the property right. The truth was that the Court acted modestly and declined to substitute its definition of "public use" for that of an elected legislature. Breyer's vision was vindicated by the popular reaction to the decision.

Insofar as the people in general, and property owners in particular, were displeased with the Court's failure to challenge the legislature and, in Monahan's words, impose a "correct" answer on the deliberative process that had led to the New London law, they were free to use the democratic process to rewrite such laws—and they did. In the 2006 elections, voters in nine states passed referenda to bar their legislatures from using the eminent domain power to transfer land between private owners.[107]

We do not suggest that this analysis of American property rights jurisprudence is even remotely exhaustive. However, it clearly indicates that the American Court has never regarded the property right as an insurmountable barrier to pursuing the collective or community interest. To the contrary, the Court has maintained throughout its history that the property right is subject to and dependent upon the preservation of the community. If the community is rendered impotent by the unfettered assertion of individual rights claims at its expense, the property right (as well as any other rights) will be rendered worthless because no community power will exist to protect the individual rights.

In fact, in one of the more celebrated decisions of the twentieth century, *United States v. Carolene Products* (1938), the Supreme Court not only struck down a due process challenge to the Filled Milk Act (which prohibited the shipment of adulterated milk in interstate commerce) but also attributed to the Congress a broad legislative authority to infringe or regulate property and economic rights.[108] In the oft-cited fourth footnote to the opinion, Justice Harlan Fiske Stone said:

> There may be narrower scope for operation of the presumption of constitutionality when legislation appears on its face to be within a specific prohibition of the Constitution, such as those of the first ten amendments, which are deemed equally specific when held to be embraced within the Fourteenth.

> It is unnecessary to consider now whether legislation which restricts those political processes which can ordinarily be expected to bring about repeal of undesirable legislation, is to be subjected to more exacting judicial scrutiny under the general prohibitions of the Fourteenth Amendment than are most other types of legislation. On restrictions upon the right to vote, on restraints upon the dissemination of information, on interferences with political organizations, [or] as to prohibition of peaceable assembly.

> Nor need we enquire whether similar considerations enter into the review of statutes directed at particular religious, or national, or racial minorities, whether prejudice against discrete and insular minorities may be a special condition, which tends seriously to curtail the operation of those political processes ordinarily to be relied upon to protect minorities, and which may call for a correspondingly more searching judicial inquiry.[109]

In this passage, the American Court relegated economic rights to second-class status while reserving the right to engage in more exacting judicial scrutiny of legislation that infringed upon rights that clearly had an impact on political participation. It resonates not only with Justice Breyer's vision of the American Constitution but also with Patrick Monahan's assertions of the need for courts to constrain individual rights in favour of the public interest and to promote democratic participation.

The Judicial Protection of Democracy: John Hart Ely's Influence and Monahan's Vision of the Community's Collective Rights

Our disagreement with Monahan's assessment of American individualism stands in contrast to our agreement with him concerning the promotion of democracy by the supreme courts of both nations. Monahan contended that the Canadian Charter was based on the promotion of democracy. In fact, he argued that the Charter reflected much of the thought of John Hart Ely, whose theory of judicial review was grounded on footnote 4 of the American Supreme Court's *Carolene Products* decision.[110]

Ely's theory charged the courts with policing the process of representation to make sure that incumbent or especially powerful political actors did not hijack the political process and, while appearing to leave it open and running smoothly, actually manipulate it to render political opposition impotent. Accordingly, Ely, Breyer, and Monahan all conceive of a judicial role that is restrained enough to allow the political process to function (and, as a result, allow the people to govern themselves democratically), yet is active enough to ensure that the political process runs fairly. The role of the judiciary in Ely's vision is to ensure that the legislation that comes out of the political process can truly be described as "popular"—not the product of bargaining among a small group of discrete interests at the expense of others.

Monahan argued that the collectivist spirit of the Charter mandated that courts refrain from using individual rights to stop the community from pursuing its collective rights and will. He said that courts should defer to the legislature (the community's voice) when it comes to making decisions about the scope and definition of rights. Judicial review, he says "should always attempt to maximize openness and the possibility of revision in social life. It should resist the impulse to freeze into place, through constitutional fiat, a particular set of economic, social and political arrangements. Rather, the goal should be to ensure that all social arrangements are subject to meaningful debate and transformation through the political process."[111]

On this basis, Monahan explained that the spirit of the Charter does indeed resonate with John Hart Ely's theory of judicial review. Yet, by Monahan's lights, the spirit of the Charter demanded more than Ely's theory offered. The first principle of the Charter, wrote Monahan, is "a right of equal access to and participation in the political process." Therefore, judicial review should "protect the basic infrastructure of liberal democracy—rights of assembly, debate and free elections. No citizen ought to be excluded from participation in the process of collective debate and argument except on compelling grounds."[112]

Monahan explained that protecting the integrity of the political process is tantamount to preserving the capacity of the polity to govern itself. If the Court steps in to "impose" the correct solution to a political dispute, it would harm the democratic deliberative process by truncating it. The result, says Monahan, would be a diminished democracy.

Judicial fiat is no substitute for ... civic deliberation. Rule by judiciary supposes that the only way to deter oppression is to impose external restraints on the political process. But, because such external restraints deny the competence of citizens to arrive at informed ethical judgments, they undermine the very process of reflection and self-criticism which might lead to a more mature collective morality. Elitist politics breeds only a mob; to produce citizens, one needs democracy.[113]

In this respect, Monahan called upon the judiciary to promote the democratic process by exercising its powers of judicial review in the same "modest" manner that Stephen Breyer advocates. As Hogg and Bushell later argued, modest (that is, dialogic) judicial review will protect the integrity of the political process and the robustness of the democracy.

The "Modest" Vision of Judicial Review and Democracy

To promote (or at least foster) the people's capacity of self-government through modesty and judicial deference, a court must clearly set forth the scope and definition of democratic rights such as access to the franchise, the exercise and meaning of the franchise, and political speech. It must also have a clear sense of what constitutes a fair basis for balancing the individual and collective aspects of those rights.

For example (as we discuss in more detail later), Monahan and Breyer both support the need for campaign spending restrictions despite the fact that they constrain political speech because they understand that unfettered individual speech may diminish the quality and diversity of speech to which the polity, collectively, is exposed. Insofar as unrestrained speech could result in the monopolization of political debate by a few powerful groups, it could debilitate the deliberative capacity of the society. Monahan and Breyer therefore acknowledge that the legislature must be granted leeway to balance the collective and individual aspects of political speech.

Accordingly, Monahan's and Breyer's modest judicial review requires courts to have a clear sense of the scope and definition of democratic rights (such as the franchise, political speech, and so forth) and an equally clear sense of what constitutes a fair democratic process. In the next three chapters, we demonstrate that within the context of election law jurisprudence, a convergence has occurred between Canadian and American judicial thought concerning the scope and definition of democratic rights. The convergence has occurred in two ways. First, insofar as the conversations among the members of both courts about issues such as campaign spending, political speech, redistribution, and prisoners' voting rights have been remarkably similar, we note that the differences emphasized by critics seem to have been overcome by the intractability of democratic rights.

Second, with regard to the role that courts should play in the regulation of the electoral process, a similar convergence has occurred. However, this convergence has come at the expense of the "modest" vision of judicial review that Monahan and Breyer support and the assumptions underlying Hogg and Bushell's dialogue. This vision assumes that the legislature can be trusted to regulate and police the democratic process fairly. That is, they assume that incumbent political powers can be trusted to regulate the process by which they are (or are not) returned to office. This, in turn, requires that legislators can overcome the self-interested tendency to erect barriers to entry and block the channels of representation that Ely said were vital to the integrity of the democratic process.

The divisions and debates in the recent campaign spending decisions of both supreme courts demonstrate that neither is completely comfortable in assuming that the legislature can rise above the conflict of interest that inheres in legislation that regulates the political marketplace. The result is a call for heightened judicial scrutiny of legislation, a solicitousness of rights claims by individuals and minority groups, and a corresponding need to balance their claims against assertions of the public interest made by the legislature.

Notes

1   The Fifth Amendment to the US Constitution provides that "[n]o person shall be ... deprived of ... property without due process of law; nor shall private property be taken for public use, without just compensation."

2   See e.g., Dennis Stone and F. Kim Walpole, "The Canadian Constitution Act and the Constitution of the United States: A Comparative Analysis," *Canadian-American Law Journal* 2 (1983): 1–36; Walter S. Tarnopolsky, "The New Canadian Charter of Rights and Freedoms as Compared and Contrasted with the American Bill of Rights," *Human Rights Quarterly* 5 (1983): 227–74; Paul Bender, "The Canadian Charter of Rights and Freedoms and the United States Bill of Rights: A Comparison," *McGill Law Journal* 28 (1983): 811–66; Drew S. Days, III, "Civil Rights in Canada: An American Perspective," *American Journal of Comparative Law* 32 (1984): 328–38.

3   Peter W. Hogg, *Constitutional Law of Canada*, 3d ed. (Toronto: Carswell, 1992), 852, note 2.

4   Roy Romanow, John Whyte, and Howard Leeson, *Canada Notwithstanding: The Making of the Constitution, 1976–1982* (Toronto: Carswell/Methuen, 1984), 245–46.

5   Alan D. Gold, "The Legal Rights Provisions—A New Vision or Deja Vu," *Supreme Court Law Review* 4 (1982): 108. According to Gold, the US Supreme Court's school

desegregation decision in *Brown v. Board of Education* (347 U.S. 483 [1954]) was "such a moral supernova in civil liberties adjudication that it almost single-handedly justifies the exercise."

6   F.L. Morton, "The Politics of Rights: What Canadians Should Know About the American Bill of Rights," *Windsor Review of Legal and Social Issues* 1 (1989): 61–96; Peter W. Hogg, "The Charter of Rights and American Theories of Interpretation," *Osgoode Hall Law Journal* 25 (1987): 87–113.

7   *Law Society of Upper Canada v. Skapinker*, [1984] 1 S.C.R. 357, 9 D.L.R. (4th) 161 at 168.

8   *Reference re s. 94(2) of the Motor Vehicle Act*, [1985] 2 S.C.R. 486, 24 D.L.R. (4th) 536 at 546.

9   *Rahey v. The Queen*, [1987] 1 S.C.R. 588 at 639.

10   *Simmons v. The Queen* (1988), 55 D.L.R. (4th) 673 at 689.

11   See Patrick Monahan, *Politics and the Constitution: The Charter, Federalism and the Supreme Court of Canada* (Toronto: Carswell, 1987); Philip L. Bryden, "The Canadian Charter of Rights and Freedoms is Antidemocratic and Un-Canadian: An Opposing Point of View," in *Crosscurrents: Contemporary Political Issues*, ed. Mark Charlton and Paul Barker (Scarborough, ON: Thompson/Nelson, 2002).

12   Mary Ann Glendon, *Rights Talk: The Impoverishment of Political Discourse* (New York: The Free Press, 1991), 161.

13   John C. Courtney, "The Franchise, Voter Registration and Electoral Districting: Who Says Canada is Just Like the United States?" (paper presented at the Annual Meeting of the American Political Science Association, Philadelphia, 2003).

14   Colin Feasby, "Issue Advocacy and Third Parties in the United Kingdom and Canada," *McGill Law Journal* 48 (2003): 11–54.

15   Janet L. Hiebert, "Elections, Democracy and Free Speech: More at Stake than an Unfettered Right to Advertise," in *Party Funding and Campaign Financing in International Perspective*, ed. K.D. Ewing and Samuel Issacharoff (Oxford: Hart Publishing, 2006), 287–88.

16   Monahan, *Politics and the Constitution*, 73.

17   Ibid., 12.

18   Ibid., 91–96.

19   Ibid., 74.

20   Alexander Bickel, *The Least Dangerous Branch: The Supreme Court at the Bar of Politics* (Indianapolis: Bobbs-Merrill, 1962); John Hart Ely, *Democracy and Distrust* (Cambridge, MA: Harvard University Press, 1980); F.L. Morton and Rainer Knopff, *The Charter Revolution & the Court Party* (Peterborough, ON: Broadview Press, 2000); and Christopher Manfredi, *Judicial Power and the Charter*, 2d ed. (New York: Oxford University Press, 2001).

21   Ibid., 88–89.

22   Alexander Hamilton, James Madison, and John Jay, *The Federalist*, Number 44, available at <http://www.constitution.org/fed/federa00.htm>.

23   Ibid.

24   Ibid., 95.

25   Ibid., 96.

26   Ronald Dworkin, *Taking Rights Seriously* (Cambridge: Harvard University Press, 1977), 269.

27   Monahan, *Politics and the Constitution*, 99.

28   Ibid.

29   See Mark Tushnet, "Policy Distortion and Democratic Debilitation: Comparative Illumination of the Countermajoritarian Difficulty," *Michigan Law Review* 94 (1995): 245–301.

30   Monahan, *Politics and the Constitution*, 99.

31   Ibid., 106.

32   Ibid., 99.

33   Ibid., 105.

34   Alexis de Tocqueville, *Democracy in America*, [1835] trans. Francis Bowen [1862] (New York: Vintage Books, 1945), 2:270.

35   Monahan, *Politics and the Constitution*,106–07.

36   Ibid., 111–12.

37   Hanna Pitkin, *The Concept of Representation* (Berkeley: University of California Press, 1967), 195.

38   Pitkin, *The Concept of Representation*, 195.

39   Monahan, *Politics and the Constitution*, 107, nr. 16; citing Jennifer Nedelsky, "Private Property and the Formation of the American Constitution."

40   See generally, Stephen Breyer, *Active Liberty: Interpreting Our Democratic Constitution* (New York: Alfred Knopf, 2005).

41   Alexander Hamilton, James Madison, and John Jay, *The Federalist*, Number 44, available at <http://www.constitution.org/fed/federa00.htm>.

42   Parts of this section are drawn from Mark Rush's review of *Active Liberty* for the Law and Politics Book Review (available at <http://www.bsos.umd.edu/gvpt/lpbr/>).

43   Breyer, *Active Liberty*, 4.

44   Breyer, "Our Democratic Constitution," Harvard University Tanner Lectures, 17–19 November 2004, available at <http://www.supremecourtus.gov/publicinfo/ speeches/sp_11-17-04.html>.

45   Ibid.

46   Breyer, *Active Liberty*, 5.

47   See generally, Joseph Bessette, *The Mild Voice of Reason: Deliberative Democracy and American National Government* (Chicago: The University of Chicago Press, 1994).

48   Monahan, *Politics and the Constitution*, 87.

49   Breyer, *Active Liberty*, 17 (internal references omitted).

50   Ibid., 5.

51   Ibid., 6.

52   Peter W. Hogg and Allison Bushell, "The *Charter* Dialogue between Courts and Legislatures (Or Perhaps the Charter of Rights Isn't Such a Bad Thing After All.)," *Osgoode Hall Law Journal* 35 (1997): 75–124.

53   Breyer, *Active Liberty*, 17.

54   *Vriend v. Alberta*, [1998] 1 S.C.R. 493, para. 130.

55   Ibid., para. 139.

56   Hogg and Bushell, "The *Charter* Dialogue."

57   Ibid., 77.

58   Ibid., 79.

59   Ibid., 92–96.

60   Ibid., 80.

61   Ibid., 82–92; *Vriend v. Alberta*, para. 137.

62   Hogg and Bushell, "The *Charter* Dialogue," 81.

63   Ibid., 105.

64   Hogg and Bushell, "The *Charter* Dialogue," 79 nr. 12. See also Louis Fisher, *Constitutional Dialogues: Interpretation as Political Process* (Princeton: Princeton University Press, 1988).

65   Hogg and Bushell, "The *Charter* Dialogue," 82, 98.

66   Ibid., 97.

67   Ibid., 101–04.

68   Hogg and Bushell, "The *Charter* Dialogue," 104–05. See *Thibaudeau v. Canada*, [1995] 2 S.C.R. 627.

69   See Allan Hutchinson, *Waiting for Coraf: A Critique of Law and Rights* (Toronto: University of Toronto Press, 1995), 184–220. Hutchinson, of course, was highly skeptical about whether the Charter could achieve this transformation.

70   Kent Roach, *The Supreme Court on Trial: Judicial Activism or Democratic Dialogue* (Toronto: Irwin Law, 2001).

71   Ibid., 54.

72   Ibid., 59.

73   See Kent Roach, "Dialogue or Defiance: Legislative Reversals of Supreme Court Decisions in Canada and the United States," *International Journal of Constitutional Law* 4 (2006): 347–70.

74   Roach, *The Supreme Court on Trial*, 60–65.

75   Ibid., 239.

76   Ibid., 251, 250.

77   Ibid., 251.

78   Hogg and Bushell, "The *Charter* Dialogue," 79, 80.

79   Ibid., 82.

80   Christopher P. Manfredi, "Judicial Power and the *Charter*: Reflections on the Activism Debate," *UNB Law Journal* 53 (2004): 185–97.

81   Matthew Hennigar, "Government Appeals as Dialogue: Expanding a Contemporary Debate" (paper presented at the Annual Meeting of the Canadian Political Science Association, Halifax, NS, 2003).

82   Martin Shapiro, "The Giving Reasons Requirement," in *On Law, Politics and Judicialization*, ed. Martin Shapiro and Alec Stone Sweet (Oxford: Oxford University Press, 2002), 228–57.

83 For a review of the early jurisprudence interpreting section 1, see Peter W. Hogg, *Constitutional Law of Canada*, 2d ed. (Toronto: Carswell, 1985), 678–90.

84 Shapiro, "The Giving Reasons Requirement," 235.

85 Ibid., 248.

86 *R. v. Oakes,* [1986] 1 S.C.R. 103 at 136.

87 Ibid., 138–40.

88 Shapiro, "The Giving Reasons Requirement," 253.

89 *R. v. Edwards Books and Art*, [1986] 2 S.C.R. 713. See Janet L. Hiebert, *Limiting Rights: The Dilemma of Judicial Review* (Montreal and Kingston: McGill-Queen's University Press, 1996), 64, 76.

90 *A.-G. Quebec v. Irwin Toy*, [1989] 1 S.C.R. 927at 993–94.

91 Ibid., 994.

92 *R. v. Keegstra*, [1990] 3 S.C.R. 697.

93 *R. v. Butler*, [1992] 1 S.C.R. 452.

94 *RJR Macdonald v. A.-G. Canada*, [1995] 3 S.C.R. 199, para. 136.

95 The others include several scholars we discuss throughout the ensuing chapters. See our following discussion of Feasby, Hiebert, and MacIvor.

96 *Charles River Bridge v. Warren*, 36 U.S. 420 (1837).

97 US Constitution, Article I, section 10.

98 *Charles River Bridge v. Warren*, 547–48.

99 Ibid., 608.

100 *Munn v. Illinois*, 94 U.S. 113 (1876).

101 Ibid., 125–26.

102 *Home Building and Loan v. Blaisdell*, 290 U.S. 398 (1934).

103 Ibid., 435.

104 *Hawaii Housing Authority v. Midkiff*, 467 U.S. 229 (1984).

105 *Kelo v. City of New London*, 125 S. Ct. 2655 (2005).

106 Ibid., 2668, citing *Berman v. Parker*, 348 U.S. 26 at 35–36.

107 See Blaine Harden, "Same-Sex Marriage, Wages Top Ballot Issues," *Washington Post*, 8 November 2006, Final Edition, sec. A, p. 36; Les Christie, "Kelo's Revenge: Voters Restrict Eminent Domain," 8 November 2006 <http://www.CNNMoney. com>.

108 *United States v. Carolene Products*, 304 U.S. 144 (1938).

109 Ibid., nr. 4.

110 John Hart Ely, *Democracy and Distrust* (Cambridge: Harvard University Press, 1980).

111 Ibid., 125.

112 Ibid., 124.

113 Ibid., 138.

chapter two

Of Real and "Self-Proclaimed" Democracies
Differing Approaches to Criminal Disenfranchisement

One area in which a majority of the Canadian Court has decided that there should be no assistance from the US experience is that of criminal disenfranchisement. In the principal cases on this issue, *Richardson v. Ramirez* and *Sauvé v. Canada*, the two courts arrived at diametrically opposite conclusions. In *Richardson v. Ramirez* (1974), a six-justice majority of the US Court held that states possess broad constitutional authority to disenfranchise persons convicted of crimes.[1] The majority based its decision on section 2 of the Fourteenth Amendment, which allows states to deny citizens the right to vote as part of the punishment "for participation in rebellion, or other crime." According to Justice William Rehnquist, the text of section 2 established an "affirmative sanction" for the "exclusion of felons from the vote" that was broad enough to justify even permanent disenfranchisement of convicted persons. Despite scholarly criticism, *Richardson* has remained settled law in the United States.[2]

At issue in *Sauvé v. Canada* (2002) (*Sauvé 2*)[3] was section 51(e) of the Canada Elections Act, which disenfranchised individuals "imprisoned in a correctional institution serving a sentence of two years or more."[4] In 1995, the trial division of the Federal Court invalidated section 51(e), but the Federal Court of Appeal reversed the decision and upheld the law by a vote of 2–1 in 1999.[5] In 2002, a closely divided Supreme Court declared section 51(e) unconstitutional by a margin of 5–4.

The Canadian Court's majority judgment in *Sauvé 2*, authored by Chief Justice Beverley McLachlin, was dismissive—to the point of hostility—toward the state of American law in this area. The chief justice's judgment did not cite, even if only to explicitly reject, *Richardson*. Moreover, she was unimpressed that other jurisdictions, especially in the United States, disenfranchise convicted criminals. "That not all *self-proclaimed* democracies adhere to ... principles of inclusiveness, equality and citizen participation," she lectured, "says little about what the Canadian vision of democracy embodied in the Charter permits" (emphasis added).[6]

The distinctive approaches to prisoner disenfranchisement articulated by Rehnquist and McLachlin provide strong support for the proposition that there are fundamental differences in the text and interpretation of rights under the US and Canadian constitutions. Yet, the discussions in both courts concerning the nature of the franchise, the nature of democracy, and the grounds on which rights can be denied were strikingly similar in tone and content. Consequently, the issue of prisoner disenfranchisement provides a good starting point for our discussion of the judicial struggle with democracy, in both senses of that term.

Prisoner Disenfranchisement in the United States: *Richardson v. Ramirez*

In *Richardson*, Justice Rehnquist relied on a close reading of the Fourteenth Amendment to uphold California's revocation of the voting rights of three ex-felons. Under normal circumstances, a state would have to demonstrate a compelling interest to justify the denial or infringement of the franchise or any other fundamental right. However, Rehnquist argued, insofar as section 2 of the Fourteenth Amendment grants an affirmative sanction to the denial of the franchise to felons, states need not demonstrate such a compelling interest.[7] Section 2 reads:

> Representatives shall be apportioned among the several States according to their respective numbers, counting the whole number of persons in each State, excluding Indians not taxed. But when the right to vote at any election for the choice of electors for President and Vice President of the United States, Representatives in Congress, the Executive and Judicial officers of a State, or the members of the Legislature thereof, is denied to any of the male inhabitants of such State, being twenty-one years of age,

and citizens of the United States, or in any way abridged, *except for participation in rebellion, or other crime*, the basis of representation therein shall be reduced in the proportion which the number of such male citizens shall bear to the whole number of male citizens twenty-one years of age in such State (emphasis added).[8]

Rehnquist acknowledged that the justifications for denying the franchise to ex-felons (e.g., rehabilitation, retributive justice, punishment) that may have informed the thinking of the Fourteenth Amendment's framers could have become outmoded.[9] He maintained, therefore, that if California or any other state were to subscribe to the more modern view that "it is essential to the process of rehabilitating the ex-felon that he be returned to his role in society as a fully participating citizen when he has completed the serving of his term" and allow former felons to vote, the Court would not discount its decision. However, he urged, it is not for the US Supreme Court "to choose one set of values over the other."[10]

In dissent, Justices Thurgood Marshall and William Brennan rejected the majority's analysis of the reasoning underpinning section 2 of the Fourteenth Amendment and argued that its interpretation should not be "shackled to the political theory of a particular era."[11] With regard to the evolution of the Court's equal protection jurisprudence, they argued that insofar as the Court had established that a state must demonstrate a compelling interest to deny a fundamental right such as the franchise, the fact that the Fourteenth Amendment contemplated denying the franchise to criminals was not an overriding consideration.[12] Marshall and Brennan also discussed the reasons a state may have to justify the disenfranchisement of criminals in order to protect some public interest. But, insofar as "the public interest ... is constantly undergoing reexamination,"[13] Marshall and Brennan asserted that there was no longer any viable justification for denying the franchise to ex-felons.

While the Court had supported criminal disenfranchisement in earlier decisions for a host of reasons grounded in different aspects of political theory, Marshall and Brennan dismissed these justifications as "dangerous" because "the public purposes asserted to be served by disenfranchisement have been found wanting in many quarters." Thus, insofar as "[t]he ballot is the democratic system's coin of the realm," conditioning its exercise "on support of the established order is to debase that currency beyond recognition."[14]

While the American Court divided over whether the evolution of democratic theory supported the disenfranchisement of felons, absent a clear constitutional mandate to strike down laws such as California's, the majority opted to adhere to a dialogic model of constitutional development and defer to the California legislature's interpretation of the Fourteenth Amendment. In contrast, the dissent would have imposed what Patrick Monahan referred to as a "just result" (i.e., a more "just" vision of democracy and criminal rehabilitation) on California.

A Different Approach? The Supreme Court Decides *Sauvé 2*

Richardson was one of several cases brought before US federal courts at the height of the prisoners' rights movement of the late 1960s and early 1970s. By upholding broad state power to disenfranchise felons—whether in custody or not—Justice Rehnquist's opinion effectively terminated this element of the movement. In Canada, by contrast, prisoners' rights advocates were relatively successful during the 1980s and 1990s in challenging provincial and federal voting restrictions, despite the fact that these Canadian restrictions only affected prison *inmates* rather than convicted persons generally.[15] Constitutional challenges to the Canada Elections Act began in earnest in 1988 and produced mixed results until a Supreme Court decision in 1993. Prisoners' rights advocates achieved trial court victories in 1988 and 1991,[16] but also lost one case in 1988.[17] At the appellate level, they lost one case in 1988,[18] but were successful twice in 1992.[19] As a result, by the end of 1992 prisoners' rights advocates had secured decisions from the Ontario Court of Appeal and the Federal Court of Appeal declaring the relevant provisions of the Canada Elections Act unconstitutional. Indeed, the Ontario court refused to even acknowledge the legitimacy of the federal government's reasons for criminal disenfranchisement, and the federal appellate court found the restriction to be "arbitrary, unfair, and based on irrational considerations."[20]

On May 27, 1993, the Supreme Court delivered its unanimous judgment in the companion cases of *Attorney-General of Canada v. Sauvé* and *The Queen v. Belczowski (Sauvé 1)*.[21] The Court found the lower court judgments in these cases so compelling as to require only a two-paragraph oral judgment affirming that it violated the right to vote, guaranteed by section 3 of the Canadian Charter, to disenfranchise "every person undergoing punishment as an inmate in any penal institution for the commission of any offence."[22] The Canadian government responded to the *Sauvé 1* decision by redrafting the Canada Elections Act to narrow the affected class of persons to inmates of federal penitentiaries who had been convicted of indictable offences.

Predictably, prisoners' rights advocates reacted to the amended legislation by filing new constitutional challenges to the Elections Act. A challenge was once again filed on behalf of Richard Sauvé, while another was filed on behalf of a group of Aboriginal inmates in Manitoba led by Sheldon McCorrister.[23] In addition to the standard voting rights arguments, these challenges advanced two novel equality rights arguments.[24] First, they argued that prisoners as a group constitute a discrete and insular minority that has been historically subjected to social, legal, and political discrimination. Second, they argued that the criminal justice system is riddled with systemic discrimination as evident in the disproportionate representation of Aboriginal Canadians in the federal inmate population.

In contrast to the *Sauvé 1* judgment, the trial court judgment in *Sauvé 2* recognized that there were important objectives underlying the inmate voting disqualification, and that the disqualification had a rational connection to those objectives. More precisely, the trial judge concluded that inmate disenfranchisement could enhance civic responsibility and respect for the rule of law, as well as the retributive component of criminal sanctions. He found, however, that the disqualification was too broad because of its blanket application to all inmates serving terms of two years or more. In his view, this was simply too blunt an instrument for achieving the federal government's objectives. Instead, he suggested that the decision to disenfranchise should be left to the discretion of sentencing judges, who could decide on a case-by-case basis whether the individual circumstances of the convicted offender warranted the additional sanction of disenfranchisement. In that way, he argued, the disqualification would only catch those inmates who actually deserved to have their right to vote suspended.

The federal government appealed this judgment to the Federal Court of Appeal, which issued its decision on October 21, 1999. Judge Allen Linden introduced his majority judgment by observing:

> This case is another episode in the continuing dialogue between courts and legislatures on the issue of prisoner voting. In 1992 and 1993, two appeal courts and the Supreme Court of Canada held that a blanket disqualification of prisoners from voting, contained in earlier legislation which was challenged, violated section 3 of the Charter and could not be saved by section 1 of the Charter. Parliament responded to this judicial advice by enacting legislation aimed at accomplishing part of its objectives while complying with the Charter.[25]

After noting that the federal government had conceded a violation of section 3, and providing a pre- and post-Charter history of prisoner disenfranchisement, Judge Linden emphasized the need for "close attention" to the particular context of the case in determining whether the limitation on voting rights was proportionate to the government's objectives.[26]

Judge Linden identified two contextual factors of some importance to the case: the statute's relationship to the regulation of the electoral process and its relationship to the exercise of the criminal law power. In both of these areas, Linden argued, Parliament is entitled to a relatively high level of judicial deference.[27] In practice, this meant that "Parliament need not examine the finest details of each and every option open to them," nor "choose the absolutely least intrusive means of achieving a legislative goal."[28] Judge Linden, along with Chief Justice Julius Isaac, thus rejected the trial judge's view that Parliament should have enacted an even narrower form of inmate disenfranchisement in which the decision would be left to the sentencing judge. In Linden's view, the objectives of the statute were simply too complex to treat it as a mere sentencing provision:

> [T]his prohibition is a hybrid which possesses elements of the criminal sanction as well as elements of civil disability based on electoral law. While it is linked to the exercise of the criminal law power, the provision also pursues valid electoral goals. With respect, the Trial Judge impoverished the provision when he reasoned that it was merely a supplementary sentencing provision. Parliament, basing itself on electoral policy, is entitled to add civil consequences to the criminal sanction in subtle, multi-dimensional ways.[29]

In the final analysis, Judge Linden reversed the trial court and found section 51(e) to be a reasonable limit on the right to vote.

By invoking Peter Hogg and Allison Bushell's concept of "dialogue" in the first paragraph of his judgment, Judge Linden situated *Sauvé 2* at the heart of one of the most important debates in Canadian constitutional theory. However, the Supreme Court would recast the notion of the dialogue when it overruled the Federal Court of Appeal.

Sauvé 2 and the Limits of Dialogue

Although the Federal Court of Appeal considered *Sauvé 2* to be a prime example of dialogue at work, the case actually offers a good illustration of the limitations of the dialogue metaphor as initially articulated by Hogg and Bushell. Most obviously, the case is one in which two of the key structural components of dialogue are missing. First, section 3 of the Charter is written in absolute rather than qualified terms. Unlike the right to be free from "unreasonable" search or seizure, for example, the right to vote is an either/or proposition. Thus, there is no opportunity for legislatures to avoid judicial nullification by entering into a litigative dialogue with courts about whether the right has, in fact, been infringed. Indeed, in one of the earlier inmate voting rights cases, a different panel of the Federal Court of Appeal described section 3 as "straightforward," "unambiguous," and in need of "no interpretation at all."[30] It is little wonder, then, that the government quickly conceded the rights violation in *Sauvé 2*.

The second missing structural component is that section 3 is exempt from the notwithstanding clause contained in section 33, thereby precluding direct legislative reversal of judicial nullification. Chief Justice McLachlin interpreted this as evidence of the "special importance accorded to the right to vote by the Charter's framers."[31] Moreover, this exemption from section 33, in her view, argued for a stringent standard of justification for inmate disenfranchisement rather than adopting an attitude of judicial deference. Ironically, since this exemption leaves the last word on voting rights to courts and precludes legislative review of judicial review—contrary to Justice Frank Iacobucci's understanding of dialogue in *Vriend*[32]—the chief justice could just as easily have interpreted the nonapplicability of section 33 as a reason for judicial caution. Indeed, the dialogue metaphor would seem to support the view that judicial deference should *increase* as the potential for dialogue diminishes.

To be sure, perhaps the most central structural component of dialogue—section 1 and the reasonable limits justification—was still present in *Sauvé 2*. Yet, the Court's ultimate resolution of the inmate disenfranchisement question illustrates the problematic—even arbitrary—nature of dialogue even under section 1. Writing for a narrow five-justice majority, Chief Justice McLachlin was dismissive of the Federal Court of Appeal's appeal to dialogue as a justification for deference. According to her, the "healthy and important promotion of a dialogue between the legislature and the courts should not be debased to a rule of 'if at first you don't succeed, try, try again.'"[33] The "you" to which the chief justice referred was obviously the legislature, and in so referring she was confirming the privileged position of the judiciary in the dialogic exchange by virtue of its power to terminate the dialogue at a moment of its choosing. This was precisely what she decided to do with respect to inmate disenfranchisement, structuring her judgment in such a way as to preclude any further legislative response to judicial nullification short of formal constitutional amendment.

The capacity of section 1 to serve as an instrument of dialogue is limited to cases where judicial nullification is based on the "least restrictive means" prong of the *Oakes* proportionality test. In these cases, governments can re-enact their legislative objectives through ordinary legislation, albeit within new parameters set by the Court. However, if legislation is nullified because its objectives are determined not to be "pressing or substantial," or because the Court fails to find a rational connection between the means and ends, then legislatures are left with severely limited or nonexistent response options. In *Sauvé 1*, the Supreme Court avoided this outcome by ignoring these components of the *Oakes* test and simply declaring that "s. 51(*e*) is drawn too broadly and fails to meet the proportionality test, particularly the minimal impairment component of the test." Similarly, the trial court in *Sauvé 2* accepted both the government's objectives and the rational connection between inmate disenfranchisement and the achievement of those objectives. Chief Justice McLachlin, however, took a very different view of these questions in her majority judgment.

The chief justice began her judgment by characterizing the dispute as one concerning "core democratic rights" rather than "competing social philosophies."[34] The judicial role under the Charter, she continued, is to uphold and maintain "an inclusive, participatory democratic framework within which citizens can explore and pursue different conceptions of the good." Courts must therefore be "vigilant in fulfilling their constitutional duty to protect the integrity of this system" when "legislative choices threaten to undermine the foundations of the participatory democracy."[35] In contrast to the lower courts, McLachlin was highly skeptical of the reasons underlying the legislative choice to disenfranchise penitentiary inmates. In her view, these reasons were not connected to the correction of any "specific problem or concern."[36]

Instead, "vague and symbolic" objectives—enhancing civic responsibility, respect for the rule of law, and the general purposes of criminal sentencing—drove the decision to disenfranchise inmates. Such "broad and abstract" objectives, the chief justice argued, are susceptible to "distortion and manipulation."[37] After articulating several reasons why such "suspect" objectives should not be considered pressing and substantial, McLachlin ultimately decided that, "despite the abstract nature of the government's objectives and the rather thin basis upon which they rest, prudence suggests that we proceed to the proportionality analysis, rather than dismissing the government's objectives outright."[38] Inmate disenfranchisement thus survived the first step in the *Oakes* test with the weakest possible judicial endorsement. However, an already skeptical chief justice became explicitly—even if respectfully—hostile when she turned to the rational connection prong of the proportionality test.

McLachlin stated the government's burden succinctly and directly: It had to demonstrate, by evidence or logic, that inmate disenfranchisement would enhance respect for the law and impose legitimate punishment.[39] She identified three theories that might serve the government's purpose in this respect: (1) that inmate disenfranchisement educates prisoners and the general public about the importance of respect for the law; (2) that inmate voting demeans the political system; and (3) that disenfranchisement is a legitimate form of punishment for any offence. She dismissed the first theory as counterproductive. Relying on logic rather than evidence, she concluded that inmate disenfranchisement communicates messages that tend to undermine, rather than enhance, respect for law and democracy. Indeed, she characterized the first theory as a "novel" one "that would permit elected representatives to disenfranchise a segment of the population." This theory, she declared, has "no place in a democracy built upon principles of inclusiveness, equality, and citizen participation."[40] Similarly, she rejected the second theory as being based on the "ancient and obsolete" idea that categories of persons could be disenfranchised because of "moral unworthiness." This idea, she stressed, "is inconsistent with the respect for the dignity of every person that lies at the heart of Canadian democracy and the *Charter*."[41]

The government's last theory fared no better in McLachlin's judgment. In her view, the argument that disenfranchisement was a legitimate component of the state's punitive arsenal failed for two reasons. First, she was not convinced that denying constitutional rights unrelated to legal rights could be used as punishment. Second, she found that inmate disenfranchisement was arbitrary and failed to promote any of the acceptable purposes of criminal sanctions (i.e., deterrence, rehabilitation, retribution, and denunciation). After stripping away the "façade of rhetoric" from this third theory, she found the untenable claim that "criminals are people who have broken society's norms and may therefore be denounced and punished as the government sees fit, even to the point of removing fundamental constitutional rights."[42] The chief justice was having none of this, and she simply rejected the argument that inmate disenfranchisement advanced lawful punishment objectives.

The chief justice's judgment elicited a particularly sharp dissent from Justice Charles Gonthier (supported by Justices Claire L'Heureux-Dubé, John Major, and Michel Bastarache). Justice Gonthier described his disagreement with McLachlin as lying at a more fundamental level than simply the immediate question of inmate disenfranchisement. In his view, the case rested "on philosophical, political and social considerations which are not capable of 'scientific proof.'"[43] There was, in other words, no compelling reason to prefer her view that temporary disenfranchisement of inmates injures the rule of law, democracy, and the right to vote over his view that the Court should defer "to Parliament's reasonable view that it strengthens these same features of Canadian society."[44] To do otherwise, he argued, would be to make judicial preferences the principal criterion for judgment under section 1 and to ignore the fact that "neither the courts nor Parliament hold a monopoly on the determination of values."[45]

Why did Justice Gonthier consider it reasonable for Parliament to conclude that inmate disenfranchisement might strengthen Canadian democracy? He began by stressing the moral purposes underlying criminal punishment, and the fact that Parliament had linked inmate disenfranchisement to serious criminal conduct. Where the chief justice saw disenfranchisement as an attack on the dignity and worth of inmates, Gonthier saw it as recognition, through punishment, of the rationality and autonomy of serious criminal offenders. Moreover, he viewed such temporary disenfranchisement as "morally educative" for inmates and the general population alike because it "reiterates society's commitment to the basic moral values which underpin the *Criminal Code*."[46] The social contract underlying the denunciation of crime, he continued, "relies upon the acceptance of the rule of law and civic responsibility and on society's need to promote the same," and to permit serious offenders to vote would undermine those two values.[47] Finally, Justice Gonthier's review of both provincial and foreign practices—including American practices—indicated that Canada's statute fell within the wide range of existing international approaches to inmate disenfranchisement.[48]

Needless to say, Justice Gonthier's *Oakes* test analysis generated a very different result from the one produced by the chief justice. In particular, he offered a more flexible understanding of the proof necessary to establish a rational connection between means and ends. Citing *RJR MacDonald*, Gonthier understood that a rational connection could be established through "reason, logic, or simply common sense."[49] In the absence of an empirically demonstrable causal relationship—in either direction—between inmate disenfranchisement and its legislative objectives, Justice Gonthier looked to whether those objectives "are at least logically furthered" by Parliament's chosen policy.[50] He answered this question in the affirmative, and reacted harshly to the chief justice's opposite view by accusing her of simply replacing "one reasonable position with another" and improperly "dismissing the government's position as 'unhelpful.'"[51]

McLachlin's view that dialogue should not be transformed into a doctrine of judicial deference seems to have been influenced by an equally sharp dissent by Justice Iacobucci in *R. v. Hall* (2002), decided only three weeks before *Sauvé 2*.[52] At issue was the constitutionality of bail provisions enacted in response to a negative judicial decision. In a 5–4 decision, the majority (led by McLachlin) found part of the new provisions unconstitutionally vague, but upheld another part as constituting an intelligible standard. In defending deference on this second point, the chief justice invoked the dialogue metaphor, arguing that *Hall* "is an excellent example of such dialogue."[53] Justice Iacobucci reacted strongly, accusing the chief justice of transforming "dialogue into abdication." He argued, "The mere fact that Parliament has responded to a constitutional decision of this Court is no reason to defer to that response where it does not demonstrate a proper recognition of the constitutional requirements imposed by that decision."[54] Chief Justice McLachlin was apparently persuaded by this argument, adopting Iacobucci's activist interpretation of dialogue in *Sauvé 2*, just as Justice Gonthier adopted the deferential interpretation for which Iacobucci had criticized her in *Hall*.

The McLachlin-Gonthier dispute in *Sauvé 2*, which was quite sharp by Canadian standards, reveals the limitations of dialogue as a formula for overcoming the inherent conflict between constitutional judicial review and democracy. Like the interpretation of "reasonable limits," the meaning of "dialogue" can vary from justice to justice. While some justices—like Iacobucci, and McLachlin in *Sauvé 2*—may view dialogue as a licence for aggressive judicial review, others—like Gonthier, and McLachlin in *Hall*—may view it as requiring judicial deference.

Reflections

We conclude this chapter with some reflections on how well the two courts dealt with the substantive question at issue in *Richardson* and *Sauvé 2*. The Canadian and American inmate disenfranchisement decisions reflect two distinctive approaches to judicial review under a liberal constitution. *Richardson* is an almost perfect illustration of modest interpretivist constitutional adjudication at work.[55] Finding textual authority for state disenfranchisement of convicted persons, which neither amendment nor precedent had superseded, Rehnquist straightforwardly concluded that states have complete discretion whether to exercise that authority or not. By contrast, in deciding that inmate disenfranchisement unreasonably limits the right to vote guaranteed to all Canadian citizens, Canadian courts have acted with what can best be described as inconsistent modesty. On the one hand, the Canadian decisions restoring the voting rights of prison inmates are a justifiable interference with the majoritarian legislative process because they prevent the exclusion of a vulnerable minority from the political process. On the other hand, the Canadian decisions that have rejected the very objectives of criminal disenfranchisement represent a moral re-evaluation of conventional ideas of justice and community membership.

The respect that the original meaning of a constitution's text acquires by virtue of its enactment by an extraordinary majority certainly provided Rehnquist with sufficient justification to defer to the California legislature and uphold the statute in *Richardson*. However, his strict adherence to, and exclusive reliance on, nineteenth-century constitutional language left the impression that the majority believed there was no other reasonable or principled basis for the policy underlying the law. He did acknowledge that states were free to pursue other justifications for enfranchising or disenfranchising former inmates. Yet, he did so only in a passing commentary at the end of his majority opinion.

Nonetheless, Rehnquist's emphasis on the original constitutional language did little to advance the notion that there was room for dialogue between the Court and the state legislatures. This is certainly evident in the scholarly reaction to *Richardson*. Consequently, strict construction of the Fourteenth Amendment allowed the *Richardson* majority to abdicate its responsibility to educate the public about the principles underlying the constitution by explaining why criminal disenfranchisement might be consistent with the norms of a good political regime.[56] To be sure, the decision did reinforce two important regime principles: respect for majority rule and adherence to the rule of law by public officials, including judges. However, it also reinforced the common criticism that majority rule is simply arbitrary, or, in the case of constitutional text, irrelevant for deciding contemporary disputes.

For their part, the decisions invalidating inmate disenfranchisement in Canada undermine the claim that a noninterpretive approach to constitutional adjudication forces courts to apply abstract moral reasoning to contemporary policy dilemmas. Such reasoning is certainly not apparent in the judicial interpretation of citizenship or the right to vote in these cases. By treating section 3 of the Charter as beyond interpretation, early decisions arguably mischaracterized the state of both political theory and Canadian constitutional doctrine. On the one hand, the meaning of citizenship has become one of the critical questions in contemporary legal and political theory, as analysts have struggled to reconcile its procedural and substantive dimensions.[57] On the other hand, the meaning of the "right to vote" was the subject of interpretation only one year prior to *Sauvé 1*, with the Court refusing to give it a narrow literal reading in the Saskatchewan electoral boundaries decision (which we take up in the next chapter). Like the US Court in *Richardson*, Canadian courts appear to have conveniently invoked constitutional text to avoid seriously considering the full range of normative principles that might be at stake in criminal disenfranchisement.

This is not to say that the decisions are without any animating normative principle at all. The noninterpretive character of the Canadian decisions is found in their "reasonable limits" analysis.[58] As discussed above, in applying the *Oakes* test, courts have expressed four broad reservations about criminal disenfranchisement. First, they have characterized the principal objectives offered for criminal disenfranchisement as unacceptably abstract and symbolic. Second, they have questioned whether there is any rational connection between criminal disenfranchisement and the achievement of any of the utilitarian objectives of criminal sanctions, such as incapacitation, deterrence, and rehabilitation. Third, they have criticized the scope of its application. Fourth, they have not found any collective benefit generated by achieving criminal disenfranchisement's objectives, emphasizing instead the negative social value produced by achieving even its retributive objectives.[59]

The principle that underlies these conclusions is decidedly utilitarian. As the 1992 Federal Court of Appeal judgment upheld by the Supreme Court in *Sauvé 1* stated, achieving the objectives of criminal disenfranchisement must "translate into some real intended benefit."[60] An even clearer statement of the principle is found in this passage from the trial court judgment in *Sauvé 2*:

> The intellectual debate among moral philosophers over the nature and purposes of punishment normally does not enter into the practical business of sentencing: rather, sentencing aims and principles seem to have a somewhat more pragmatic focus. Indeed, there may be strong philosophic and political reasons to support the disenfranchisement of prisoners; however, there appears [*sic*] to be few practical reasons for doing so.[61]

To be sure, the imposition of criminal punishment aims at the practical goal of protecting persons and property by reducing crime. However, it also has an important expressive element, which serves "to reaffirm the common moral sentiment of the community."[62] By depreciating this normative justification for punishment, the Canadian decisions illustrate that noninterpretive judicial review does not necessarily represent the substitution of principle for expedience.

Conclusion

Our analysis of the two courts' decisions concerning criminal disenfranchisement demonstrates that the contrasts between the two nations are not as stark as some observers suggest. Certainly, *Sauvé* and *Richardson* produced opposite results. However, the two courts engaged in essentially the same debates about the scope and definition of, as well as access to, the franchise. Some members of both courts respectfully disagreed with, but still deferred to, the respective legislature's justifications for disenfranchising criminals. Other court members would have struck down the disenfranchisement provisions because they disagreed with the political and theoretical visions underlying the legislature's justification for adopting those provisions. In both cases, had some court members retired and been replaced, the two courts might have arrived at similar conclusions.

We see a similar pattern in the two supreme courts' approaches to redistribution of legislative seats, campaign spending restrictions, and political speech. This leads us to our two principal conclusions. First, the US and Canadian courts really have converged, both in the manner in which they debate issues of election law and democratic rights and in the way that they decide challenges to electoral legislation. Second, these cases demonstrate a gradual, yet continuous, erosion of the premises and assumptions underpinning the dialogic view of constitutional interpretation and development.

Notes

1   *Richardson v. Ramirez*, 418 U.S. 24 (1974).

2   Laurence Tribe, *American Constitutional Law* (Mineola, NY: Foundation Press, 1978), 771–72; Note, "The Disenfranchisement of Ex-Felons: Citizenship, Criminality, and the 'Purity of the Ballot Box,'" *Harvard Law Review* 102 (1989): 1300–17.

3   *Sauvé v. Canada*, [2002] 3 S.C.R. 519. Hereafter cited as *Sauvé 2*. In the interests of full disclosure, readers should know that Christopher Manfredi served as an expert witness for the Government of Canada in this case.

4   *Canada Elections Act*, R.S.C. 1985, c. E-2, s. 51(e), as amended by S.C. 1993, c. 19, s. 23. In effect, this meant that only inmates of federal penitentiaries would be affected by the voting restriction, since sentences of less than two years are served in provincial prisons and/or jails.

5   *Sauvé and McCorrister v. Canada*, [1996] 1 F.C. 857 (F.C.T.D.); *Sauvé and McCorrister v. Canada*, [2000] 2 F.C. 117 (F.C.A.).

6   *Sauvé 2*, para. 41.

7   *Richardson v. Ramirez*, 54.

8   US Constitution, Article 14, section 2.

9   *Richardson v. Ramirez*, 55.

10   Ibid.

11   Ibid., 76.

12   Ibid., 77–78.

13   Ibid., 82.

14   Ibid., 83.

15   One exception to this characterization of these restrictions was the British Columbia Elections Act, which applied broadly to "persons serving their sentences." Consequently, probationers and parolees not in prison were disenfranchised. See Rainer Knopff and F.L. Morton, *Charter Politics* (Toronto: Nelson, 1992), 293.

16   *Badger v. Canada* (1988), 55 Man. R. (2d) 211 (Man. Q.B.); *Belczowski v. Canada*, [1991] 3 F.C. 151 (F.C.T.D.).

17   *Sauvé v. A.-G. Canada* (1988), 66 O.R. (2d) 234 (Ont. H.C.J.).

18   *Badger v. Canada* (1988), 55 Man. R. (2d) 198 at 204–205 (Man. C.A.).

19   *Belczowski v. Canada*, [1992] 2 F.C. 440 (F.C.A.); *Sauvé v. Canada (Attorney General)* (1992), 7 O.R. (3d) 481 (Ont. C.A.).

20   *Belczowski v. Canada*, [1992] 2 F.C. 440 (F.C.A.).

21   *Attorney-General of Canada v. Sauvé*, [1993] 2 S.C.R. 438. Hereafter cited as *Sauvé 1*.

22   *Canada Elections Act*, R.S.C. 1985, c. E-2, s. 51(e). Section 3 of the Charter declares that "[e]very citizen of Canada has the right to vote in an election of members of the House of Commons or of a legislative assembly and to be qualified for membership therein."

23   *Sauvé v. Chief Electoral Officer of Canada et al.*; *McCorrister et al. v. Attorney General of Canada* (1995), 132 D.L.R. (4th) 136 (F.C.T.D.). Hereafter cited as *Sauvé/McCorrister*.

24   Although an equality rights argument had been raised (and rejected) in *Belczowski* ([1991] 3 F.C. 151 at 162), the arguments presented in *Sauvé/McCorrister* were far more systematic and sophisticated.

25   *Sauvé and McCorrister v. Canada*, [2000] 2 F.C. 117 at para. 56 (F.C.A.).

26   Ibid., para. 88.

27   Ibid., para. 115.

28   Ibid., para. 121.

29   Ibid., para. 129.

30   *Belczowski v. Canada*, [1992] 2 F.C. 440 at 452 (F.C.A.).

31   *Sauvé 2*, para. 11.

32   *Vriend v. Alberta*, [1998] 1 S.C.R. 493 at paras. 137, 139. See also endnote 57 and the accompanying text in Chapter 1 of this book.

33   *Sauvé 2*, para. 17.

34   Ibid., para. 13.

35   Ibid., para. 15.

36   Ibid., para. 21.

37   Ibid., para. 22.

38   Ibid., para. 26.

39   Ibid., para. 28.

40 Ibid., para. 41.

41 Ibid., para. 44.

42 Ibid., para. 52.

43 Ibid., para. 67.

44 Ibid., para. 68.

45 Ibid., para. 104.

46 Ibid., paras. 73, 75.

47 Ibid., paras. 115–16.

48 Ibid., paras. 122–34.

49 Ibid., para. 150; citing *RJR MacDonald*, para. 86.

50 Ibid., para. 151.

51 Ibid., para. 157; citing the chief justice at para. 37.

52 *R. v. Hall*, [2002] 3 S.C.R. 309.

53 Ibid., para. 43.

54 Ibid., para. 127.

55 "Interpretivism." refers to judicial review of legislation based only on a close reading of the constitutional text. "Noninterpretivism" refers to the practice of relying on extraconstitutional sources (e.g., the American Declaration of Independence) in addition to constitutional ones to decide whether to uphold or strike down challenged legislation. See, e.g., John Hart Ely's discussion in *Democracy and Distrust* (Cambridge, MA: Harvard University Press, 1980).

56 See Ralph Lerner, "The Supreme Court as Republican Schoolmaster," in *The Supreme Court Review*, ed. Philip Kurland (Chicago: University of Chicago Press, 1967), 127–80; Ralph A. Rossum, "The Supreme Court as Republican Schoolmaster: Freedom of Speech, Political Equality, and the Teaching of Political Responsibility," in *Taking the Constitution Seriously: Essays on the Constitution and Constitutional Law*, ed. Gary McDowell (Dubuque, IA: Kendall/Hunt, 1981), 125–38; Charles H. Franklin and Liane C. Kosaki, "Republican Schoolmaster: The U.S. Supreme Court, Public Opinion, and Abortion," *American Political Science Review* 83 (1989): 751–71.

57 For a survey, see Will Kymlicka and Wayne Norman, "Return of the Citizen: A Survey of Recent Work on Citizenship Theory," *Ethics* 104 (1994): 360–69.

58 An interpretivist approach to section 3 would accept as "reasonable" all limits that predated the Charter (i.e., that existed prior to 1982). The Canadian decisions are noninterpretivist not because of any novel meaning attached to the concepts of "citizenship" or "right to vote" but because of the meaning attached to the concept of "reasonable limit."

59 *Sauvé/McCorrister*, 176.

60 *Belczowski v. Canada*, [1992] F.C. 440 at 457 (F.C.A.).

61 *Sauvé/McCorrister*, 174.

62 Roger Scruton, *A Dictionary of Political Thought* (London: Pan Books, 1983), 388.

chapter three

The Scope and Definition of the Franchise

Chief Justice Beverley McLachlin's dismissal of American jurisprudence in *Sauvé 2* echoed her earlier dismissal of US doctrine in the Canadian Court's first voting rights case, *Reference re Provincial Electoral Boundaries (Sask.)* (the *Saskatchewan Reference*) (1991).[1] At issue was whether provincial electoral boundaries infringed section 3 of the Charter because of population discrepancies that advantaged rural over urban electoral districts. This issue brought to Canada a controversy with which the US Supreme Court had been grappling since the early 1960s. In *Baker v. Carr* (1962) and *Reynolds v. Sims* (1964), the US Court had established the standard of "one person, one vote."[2] Writing in *Reynolds*, Chief Justice Earl Warren declared that "[l]egislators represent people, not trees or acres. Legislators are elected by voters, not farms or cities or economic interests.... Overweighting and overvaluation of the votes of those living here has the certain effect of dilution and undervaluation of the votes of those living there."[3]

In Justice McLachlin's view, this rigid standard was both undesirable and radical.[4] Indeed, she suggested that the argument in favour of importing the American standard to Canada depended on an overly narrow interpretation of the "right to vote." Instead, she determined that the right protected by section 3 of the Charter "is not equality of voting power per se, but the right to 'effective representation.'"[5] To be sure, she recognized that "relative parity of voting power" constituted an important condition of effective representation, but she asserted that it is insufficient for two reasons. First, it is impossible to achieve absolute parity. Second, even if this were possible, an exclusive focus on the individual right to equal voting power would miss important collective factors such as "geography, community history, community interests and minority representation."[6]

Like *Sauvé 2*, this electoral boundaries decision provides traction for discussing differences in Canadian and American election law decisions. Scholars generally agree that American voting rights jurisprudence has gone through three "generations" of development.[7] First generation voting rights issues concerned individual equality: access to the polls, equality of voting power, and so on. The American Court's early reapportionment decisions and the first focus of the Voting Rights Act (VRA) addressed this aspect of voting. Second generation issues concerned group issues such as vote dilution and racial or partisan gerrymandering. These issues were the focus of sections 2 and 5 of the VRA and the controversies concerning minority vote dilution.[8] Currently, third generation issues deal with "governance" or the manner in which the political process is conducted after ensuring that access to the ballot and opportunities for representation are protected. Third generation issues address whether the rules governing the legislative process actually allow minority groups and voters to have a fair chance to influence (and sometimes win) legislative deliberations.[9]

The Canadian and American courts have, for the most part, engaged in balancing first and second generation claims. Both courts have maintained the importance of individual voting equality, but both have also acknowledged that fair and effective group representation may require some deviation from the individualistic ideal. Trying to balance the competing group and individual claims has proven to be a Herculean and controversial task. The balancing has come about differently in the two countries.

In the United States, the balancing of individual and group voting rights has taken place in phases and in the heated context of the affirmative action debate. The Court first established the one-person-one-vote principle of individual voting equality in early decisions such as *Baker v. Carr, Reynolds v. Sims*, and *Lucas v. Forty-Fourth General Assembly of Colorado* (1964).[10] The one-person-one-vote principle was not cast at the expense of particular conceptions of group voting rights. Instead, it was cast in terms of ensuring majority rule (that is, that electoral majorities produce legislative majorities) and in terms of equal protection of the laws, particularly with regard to how and whether the law discriminates among voters on the basis of where they live.

At the same time, the Court also confronted questions concerning the scope of the franchise. In *Allen v. State Board of Elections* (1969), it was asked to rule on the meaning of an "electoral practice" as set forth in section 5 of the VRA.[11] Acknowledging that the one-person-one-vote rule would do little to protect the rights of minority voters to gain access to the polls and to gain effective representation, the Supreme Court interpreted section 5 of the VRA broadly, thereby taking the first steps toward conceiving of the franchise in terms of more than simple equality of individual voting power.[12]

The US Court first confronted group representation rights in cases concerning the requirements posed by section 2 of the VRA as it was amended in 1982. This injected a tension into the Court's voting jurisprudence.[13] In passing the VRA, Congress imposed a new set of constraints (protection of minority representational opportunities) on state legislatures that they had to take into account—along with the Court's one-person-one-vote ruling—when redrawing their legislative district boundaries.

The protection of minority interests does not inherently conflict with the preservation of equal individual voting power. However, since minority populations are not always geographically concentrated, states must draw bizarrely shaped districts in order to promote minority representational opportunities while adhering to the one-person-one-vote standard. This was controversial because the creation of such bizarre districts clearly demonstrated that the districts had been drawn with the sole purpose of conditioning the electoral process in order to enhance the likelihood of particular results—the election of minority candidates. The resistance of some members of the Court to this practice was not cast in terms of the one-person-one-vote principle because, in drawing such districts, state legislatures usually conform to it (or at least they do not deviate very far from it). Instead, opponents said that the drawing of such special-interest districts violated the right to cast a *meaningful* vote in an electoral process whose outcomes were not preconditioned and therefore not rendered illegitimate by considerations of race.

The VRA thus presented a conundrum for the American Court that did not exist in Canada. The Fourteenth Amendment to the American Constitution speaks only in terms of "equal protection of the laws." It makes no exceptions or special reservations for particular minority groups. It is read by some members of the Court (such as Justices Antonin Scalia and Clarence Thomas) as an outright ban on any legislative consideration of race. In contrast, section 15 of the Charter requires governments to take group interests into account.

Accordingly, in the *Saskatchewan Reference*, the Canadian Court dispensed with the one-person-one-vote issue and embraced group representation rights in an unremarkable fashion. Yet, the Court was divided as several justices (and some scholars) criticized the Court for forsaking the one-person-one-vote rule.[14] Nevertheless, the decision was certainly in keeping with the letter, if not the spirit, of the Charter.[15] In contrast, the US equal protection clause's failure to make exceptions for the rights of particular groups ensured that the American Court would endure a divisive controversy as it tried to reconcile the VRA's call to accommodate the interests of racial minorities with the equal protection clause's commitment to individual equality.

In the end, however, the American Court's voting rights jurisprudence echoes the concerns and conclusions of its Canadian neighbour. Over the course of the 1990s, the American Court confronted a series of equal protection challenges to the creation of districts drawn to enhance the representational opportunities of candidates who were members of racial and ethnic minorities. The Court first stated in *Shaw v. Reno* (1993) that the creation of so-called majority-minority districts posed an important equal protection problem, even though they appeared to be sanctioned by the VRA.[16] However, it gradually moderated its position and granted states more leeway in creating them. This shift paralleled a similar moderation of the Court's affirmative action jurisprudence in other areas.

American Jurisprudence: Individualistic Foundations?

The American Court first encountered the issue of individual voting equality with regard to redistricting in *Colegrove v. Green* (1946).[17] There, the Court affirmed the lower federal court's dismissal of a challenge to Illinois's congressional district boundaries. The plaintiffs had asserted that the districting scheme—which had not been changed since 1901—was unconstitutional because the vast differences in district populations resulted in inequalities of individual voting power.

The Court ruled that reapportionment issues were inherently "political questions" that were most appropriately left to the legislative branch and/or the political processes to resolve. Nonetheless, the justices divided regarding the basis on which to dismiss the complaint. While Justice Felix Frankfurter (who wrote the opinion of the Court) emphasized the political nature of the reapportionment question, Justice Wiley Rutledge contended that the appeal should have been dismissed for a want of equity.

Rutledge noted that the right to vote is not absolute.[18] Furthermore, he argued that the Constitution offered no guidance concerning the scope and definition of the franchise. He therefore agreed with Justice Frankfurter that judicial meddling with questions of reapportionment was, in his words, a cure worse than the disease (of malapportioned congressional districts).[19] Absent a clear constitutional mandate, striking down a legislative apportionment scheme that was not based on the one-person-one-vote principle merely substituted the preferred political theory of five Supreme Court justices for that of the state legislature.

In dissent, Justice Hugo Black (joined by Justices Frank Murphy and William Douglas) asserted that the malapportionment of legislative districts presented a clear violation of the Fourteenth Amendment's equal protection clause. While, as Rutledge noted, the scope of the right to vote may not have had any clear or absolute interpretation, Black urged that this did not empower states to administer elections in an arbitrary or discriminatory manner. As Black saw it, there was no principled difference between electoral districts with minor population variations and an apportionment scheme that would allow the citizens of one county to elect all of the members of a state's congressional delegation.[20] Inequality of voting power was inequality of voting power, period.

The divisions in *Colegrove* were quite instructive. Insofar as the dissent conceived of the franchise in terms of equality of voting power, they did not concern themselves with the problems of equity raised by the majority of the Court. In this respect, however, it is important to note that the dissent therefore saw reapportionment as an *equal protection* issue—not an issue specifically regarding voting rights. Accordingly, the dissent also did not see themselves as imposing any particular democratic theory upon the states. Instead, they sought only to prevent capricious discrimination—regardless of whether a particular substantive right was at stake—in a discrete area of public policy.

When it decided *Baker v. Carr*, the Court had experienced a change of personnel and a change of mind. In *Baker*, the Court heard a challenge to the apportionment of state legislative districts in Tennessee, which had not redrawn its legislative districts since 1901. As a result of the gross population disparities that had developed among legislative and senatorial districts, it had become possible for 37 per cent of the voters to elect 20 of the 33 members of the state senate and 40 per cent of the voters to elect 63 of the 99 members of the house. The representation and voting power across different counties was characterized by huge disparities. For example, Moore

County, with a population of 2,340, had the same number of representatives as Rutherford County, which had 25,316 residents.

Speaking for the Court, Justice William Brennan stated that reapportionment entailed a straightforward issue of equal protection. Absent any rational justification for the systemic inequalities of voting power, there was no basis for sustaining the apportionment scheme. Most of the decision was dedicated to establishing whether the Court had the capacity to rule on such a "political question." Even among the concurrences, there was great concern about whether the Court could fashion an effective and unassailable remedy for malapportionment cases. Fortunately, the actual focus of the decision was quite narrow. As Justice Brennan asserted, "[W]e hold today only (a) that the court possessed jurisdiction of the subject matter; (b) that a justiciable cause of action is stated upon which appellants would be entitled to appropriate relief; and (c) because appellees raise the issue before this Court, that the appellants have standing to challenge the Tennessee apportionment statutes."[21]

In dissent, Justices Frankfurter and John Harlan regarded the decision as much more ominous. They reasserted that reapportionment was a political question that embodied issues beyond the scope of the Court's capacity and competence. First, Frankfurter asserted that there was a qualitative and constitutional difference between claims of vote denial brought under the Fifteenth and Nineteenth Amendments and claims of inequality of voting power brought under the Fourteenth. Whereas the Fifteenth and Nineteenth Amendments explicitly forbade vote *denial*, the Fourteenth made no reference to *equality of voting power*. Frankfurter argued that American and British history indicated a clear disposition *not* to use population as the exclusive basis for representation.[22]

As we note above, Frankfurter concluded that there was neither a historical basis nor a clear constitutional mandate for the Court to infer that the Fourteenth Amendment required equality of individual voting power. Thus, while the majority of the Court avoided the problem of fashioning a remedy for malapportionment (by remanding the case to the lower court), Frankfurter contended that the Court was merely putting off the inevitable. Once the Court established that apportionment was a justiciable issue, it ensured that whatever remedy a lower court fashioned would be subject to challenge. This inevitably would return the issue to the Supreme Court and force it to either affirm a lower court's remedy or fashion one of its own.

In *Reynolds v. Sims*, the inevitable occurred.[23] *Reynolds* embodied a challenge to a provisional reapportionment scheme that had been drafted by the federal district court in Alabama. In the wake of *Baker*, citizens had challenged the existing apportionment of the Alabama legislature which—as had been the case in Tennessee—had not been changed for some 60 years and, as a result, embodied districts with gross disparities between populations. The Alabama legislature proposed two new apportionment schemes, but the federal district court in Alabama rejected both because neither came close to resolving the gross population disparities that had previously existed. The district court then called for new elections under a provisional apportionment scheme that it had drafted.

Chief Justice Warren sought to elaborate and clarify the Court's vision of the right to vote, as well as its conception of fair and effective representation. The Supreme Court sustained the lower court's rejection of the malapportioned legislative districts. As the following discussion indicates, however, what began as a straightforward endorsement of representation on the basis of equal population ("rep by pop") transformed into a discussion of the nuances of group representation.

In contrast to Frankfurter's argument in *Baker v. Carr*, Warren asserted that the American conception of the franchise would be based on the one-person-one-vote principle. Thus, Warren established unequivocally—or so it seemed—that the franchise was grounded on equality of individual voting power. Insofar as the franchise was regarded as a fundamental right and defined in terms of "one person, one vote," a state could infringe on it (by deviating from equality of individual voting power) only if it demonstrated a compelling reason for doing so.

Yet Warren qualified his description almost immediately. He noted that circumstances had forced states to deviate from the one-person-one-vote standard throughout American history. Nonetheless, he maintained that such deviations were and would have to be based on compelling state interests: "So long as the divergences from a strict population standard are based on legitimate considerations incident to the effectuation of a rational state policy, some deviations from the equal-population principle are constitutionally permissible with respect to the apportionment of seats in either or both of the two houses of a bicameral state legislature."[24]

The latter part of Warren's opinion seems to contradict the former. By his reasoning, equality of voting power implies equality of representational opportunity. Yet, he later acknowledged the need to account for interests that would be harmed by a strict adherence to population equality. As a result, while he distinguished between "fair and effective representation" and equality of voting power, he did not clarify how the two are related.

Thus, Warren seemed to balance equality of voting power clearly with the need for "fair and *effective* representation." If voters cannot use the franchise to change governments, then elections are rendered a meaningless ritual and elected representatives have that much less legitimacy. Accordingly, the enforcement of the one-person-one-vote rule can be regarded as the Court's attempt to preserve the legitimacy of the entire electoral process, as well as the equality of the impact of individual votes.

This interpretation, however, is belied by the decision rendered in a companion case to *Reynolds*: *Lucas v. Forty-Fourth General Assembly of Colorado*. Here the Court struck down a Colorado state legislative redistricting plan that had been approved by initiative by a majority of the *voters* in every county in the state. The apportionment plan was designed to ensure that certain rural areas retained representation in the state legislature. The plan, however, necessitated an under-representation of urban voters. Denver area residents therefore challenged the apportionment scheme because the population disparities between the districts would allow—under the right circumstances—29.8 per cent of the state's voters to elect a majority of the lower house and 32.1 per cent of the voters to elect a majority of the upper house in the state legislature.

In *Lucas*, Warren elaborated upon his opinion in *Reynolds*. The one-person-one-vote rule was not just a mathematically simple and enforceable standard. Instead, it manifested the Court's concerns about a broader individual right to participate in a fair political process. Despite the fact that a majority of the voters supported the Colorado districting scheme, the Court nonetheless ruled that the voting right—conceived in terms of one person, one vote—simply could not be debased. Thus, the Court regarded the equally weighted vote in the same terms as any other fundamental right: Absent a compelling legislative rationale, the right could not be infringed.[25]

Lucas forces us to ponder the harm that the American Court wished to prevent by creating the one-person-one-vote standard. John Hart Ely argued that it was nothing more than a judicial artifice designed to simplify voting rights law.[26] Adherence to the one-person-one-vote rule would remove one prima facie basis on which to claim that the integrity of the electoral process (and the prospect of majority rule) had been compromised because of the unequal treatment of voters.

Other scholars such as Samuel Issacharoff and Richard Pildes suggest that another less individualistic concern underpinned the Warren Court's apportionment decisions. Insofar as legislators could design districts in a manner that would allow a minority of the voters to control a majority of the legislative seats, they could also entrench themselves into power—even if a majority of voters wished to remove them. Issacharoff and Pildes describe this Orwellian scenario as a political "lockup."[27] In *Lucas*, the Court acknowledged this possibility.

Accordingly, while the thrust of the Warren Court's early reapportionment decisions was to emphasize the importance of one person, one vote, the discussions embodied in those decisions indicate that the Court's vision was more complex than a simple commitment to ensuring equality of individual voting power. The Court acknowledged that fair and effective representation entailed more than mere individual equality. Yet, it also recognized that deviating from this standard posed the threat not only of minority rule but also of incumbent entrenchment.

Canada: The *Saskatchewan Reference*

In Canada, the debate about the scope of the franchise has also occurred with regard to the predominance and desirability of the one-person-one-vote concept. However, the Canadian groundwork differs in important ways from that in the United States.[28]

While several redistribution cases have been heard in lower courts,[29] the Canadian Supreme Court has heard only one case under the Charter: the *Saskatchewan Reference*. This concerned a challenge to the distribution of electoral boundaries in the provincial legislature under the Representation Act of 1989. The question was whether the differences in riding populations infringed upon the right to vote as it was enshrined in section 3 of the Charter. A divided Court arrived at what appears to be a completely opposite conclusion to that of the American Court in *Reynolds* and *Lucas*. Speaking for the Court, Justice McLachlin overturned a decision by the Saskatchewan Court of Appeal in which the provincial electoral distribution had been declared unconstitutional due to the population differences among the districts.

The Saskatchewan Court of Appeal had stated that one of the basic aims of legislative apportionment "must be fair and effective representation of all citizens." Therefore, "the controlling and dominant consideration in drawing electoral constituency boundaries must be voter population in the Province."[30] The appeals court concluded that any population deviation from one district to the next must be minimal and that ridings must adhere as closely as possible to the principle of one person, one vote.

The Supreme Court split with regard to the meaning of the franchise as it is set forth in section 3 of the Charter. Section 3 reads: "Every citizen of Canada has the right to vote in an election of the members of the House of

Commons or of a legislative assembly and to be qualified for membership therein." While the dissent urged that the section required equality of voting power, the majority ruled that it embodied a more expansive conception of the franchise—one that included representational opportunity as well as individual voting equality. As noted earlier in this chapter, Justice McLachlin stated: "[T]he purpose of the right to vote enshrined in s. 3 of the Charter is not equality of voting power per se, but the right to 'effective representation.'"[31]

Thus, while the Canadian Court echoed Justice Warren's assertions in *Reynolds* about fair and effective representation, it deviated from the American Court in one important respect. Whereas the American Court established "one person, one vote" as the basic principle of American reapportionment and its conception of the franchise, the Canadian Court did not. In fact, Justice McLachlin contrasted the American approach to the franchise with the "less radical, more pragmatic approach" developed in England and in Canada.[32]

McLachlin did acknowledge that the first condition of effective representation is "relative parity of voting power." However, she immediately qualified that statement by deeming absolute equality "impossible." While relative voter parity is attainable, she maintained that it could prove "undesirable" because

> it has the effect of detracting from the primary goal of effective representation. Factors like geography, community history, community interests and minority representation may need to be taken into account to ensure that our legislative assemblies effectively represent the diversity of our social mosaic. These are but examples of considerations which may justify departure from absolute voter parity in the pursuit of more effective representation; the list is not closed.[33]

The problem, of course, was to determine what constituted a legitimate basis for deviating from voter parity. Citing the lower court opinion she wrote in *Dixon v. British Columbia* (1989) prior to her elevation to the Supreme Court,[34] McLachlin explained that such deviations could be justified only "on the grounds of practical impossibility or the provision of more effective representation."[35]

Thus, in the *Saskatchewan Reference*, the Canadian Court consciously sought to avoid what it regarded as the rigid formalism of the American one-person-one-vote standard. However, in dissent, Justice Peter Cory (joined by Chief Justice Antonio Lamer and Justice Claire L'Heureux-Dubé) noted that much more was at stake than simply relaxing a mathematically rigid conception of the franchise. Cory found the challenged distribution unacceptable because it contained variations in excess of 15 per cent from the provincial quotient.

In addition, Cory argued that the constraints on the redistribution process set forth in the Representation Act (requiring specific numbers of urban and rural ridings) led to unnecessarily broad population variances. He therefore asserted that the process leading up to the redistribution, not the actual result itself, was quite troublesome: "[W]hile the actual distribution map may appear to have achieved a result that is not too unreasonable, I am of the view that the effect of the statutory conditions has been to interfere with the rights of urban voters."[36] The imposition of a specific quota of urban and rural ridings discriminated against urban interests, which, as a result of the rural riding quotas, were under-represented.

Accordingly, Cory's concern for urban voters in Saskatchewan echoed the American Court's concerns in *Lucas*. The Canadian dissent and the American majority rejected the concerns about ensuring rural representation expressed by Saskatchewan's Representation Act and the voters of Colorado, respectively. To the extent that the act called for the preservation of rural communities of interest, it did, for all intents and purposes, call for the "gerrymandering" of the political process, insofar as it endorsed the conscious attempt to condition electoral outcomes. Cory therefore argued that when the Canadian Court sustained the constitutionality of such deviations, it essentially constitutionalized gerrymandering.

The fundamental right to vote should not be diminished without sound justification. To water down the importance and significance of an individual's vote is to weaken the democratic process. Here no sound basis has been put forward to justify legislation which clearly has the effect of diminishing the rights of urban voters and reducing the representation of urban residents in the legislature. Democracy can all too easily be eroded by diluting voters' rights and representation. Voting is far too important and precious a right to be unreasonably and unnecessarily diluted.[37]

Thus, if legislatures could condition the process by which the franchise is reconstituted, it creates the possibility for a systemic debasement of the vote of some political actors.

Looking at the two supreme courts' first experiences with matters of legislative redistribution and the question of individual voting equality, it does indeed seem that they took radically divergent paths concerning the franchise. In *Baker*, *Reynolds*, and *Lucas*, the American Court split 7–2, 8–1, and 7–2 (respectively) in favour of the one-person-one-vote principle. In contrast, the Canadian Court split 6–3 against it in the *Saskatchewan Reference*. Despite the contrary results, however, it is important to note that the debates in the two courts embodied identical differences of opinion about how best to balance concerns about effective representation with individual voting equality. Furthermore, after the original one-person-one-vote decisions, the American Court gradually, yet consistently, softened its adherence to the standard in order to accommodate concerns about the effective representation of collective and group interests.

The Evolution (or Canadianization?) of American Voting Rights Jurisprudence

Despite ongoing claims about the centrality of the one-person-one-vote standard in American jurisprudence, it is clear from a complete reading of Chief Justice Warren's opinion in *Reynolds* that it is hardly the bedrock principle that some scholars—or some Supreme Court justices, for that matter—would suggest. Absolute voter equality is by no means a uniform rule of electoral organization in the United States. While requiring that congressional districts within each state be equipopulous, reapportionment results in significant population deviations among congressional districts from different states.[38] Also, while the Court has required absolute population equality in the creation of congressional districts,[39] it applies a much looser standard to the creation of state legislative districts.[40] Furthermore, in cases arising under the VRA, the American Court did acknowledge that the effective exercise of the franchise could entail the promotion of group representational opportunities, as well as protection of individual equality rights.

In the 1990s, the American Court confronted the issue of ensuring meaningful group representation rights when it was forced to reconcile the creation of majority-minority voting districts ("benign" gerrymandering of the electoral system to enhance minority representational opportunity as mandated by the VRA) with the demands of the equal protection clause. The American Court's attempt to resolve the dilemma posed by such benign gerrymandering forced it to address the dangers posed by granting the legislature the power to organize voters and political competition in a manner that would enhance the likelihood of particular electoral outcomes. Since this same power could be used to regulate political competition, enhance the likelihood of particular outcomes in election contests, and insulate incumbents from political challenges, it threatened to diminish the quality and integrity of the democratic process while simultaneously enhancing the representation opportunities of minority groups. The Court therefore had to determine whether and how the integrity of the franchise could be diminished in the name of enhancing other social goals, such as effective representation of minority interests.

Effective Representation and the VRA

The American Court first broadened the scope of the franchise in *Allen v. State Board of Elections*. *Allen* was actually the combination of several cases in which African-American voters had charged that new electoral laws passed by several Southern states required preclearance by the Justice Department. In part, this entailed a debate about the definition of the franchise. The states defined the right to vote essentially as access to the polls—and nothing more. They therefore argued that since the challenged changes to the electoral law had no impact on African-American voters' access to the polls, they were not covered by the VRA. The challenged laws included:

- ▸ a 1966 Mississippi law that allowed counties to change the manner in which their boards' supervisors were elected. Instead of using districts, they could now use at-large elections;
- ▸ another Mississippi law that allowed the boards of education in 11 counties to appoint their superintendent of education (instead of electing the superintendent);
- ▸ a Mississippi law that changed the requirements for independent candidates running in general elections;
- ▸ a Virginia law that changed the requirements for casting write-in ballots.

Siding with the plaintiffs, the Court ruled that the franchise included more than mere access to the polls. Accordingly, the Court declared that section 5 of the VRA applied to (and required federal preapproval for) these sorts of changes to electoral law. In so ruling, the Supreme Court broadened the scope of the right to vote. Speaking for the Court, Justice Warren argued:

The Voting Rights Act was aimed at the subtle, as well as the obvious, state regulations which have the effect of denying citizens their right to vote because of their race. Moreover, compatible with the decisions of this Court, the Act gives a broad interpretation to the right to vote, recognizing that voting includes "all action necessary to make a vote effective." We are convinced that in passing the Voting Rights Act, Congress intended that state enactments such as those involved in the instant cases be subject to the 5 approval requirements.[41]

While *Allen* expanded the definition of the franchise by expanding the list of "practices" that constituted "voting," Congress expanded the definition of an "infringement" of the franchise when it amended parts of the VRA in 1982. Most important, Congress altered section 2 of the VRA to allow litigants to challenge any voting scheme that had the *effect* of diluting minority voting strength—regardless of whether or not it had been established with the intent of doing so.

In *Thornburg v. Gingles* (1986), the Court affirmed this expansion of the notion of vote dilution.[42] Speaking for the Court, Justice Brennan set forth the grounds on which a minority group recognized by the VRA could claim that its representation rights had been infringed:

> First, the minority group must be able to demonstrate that it is sufficiently large and geographically compact to constitute a majority in a single-member district.... Second, the minority group must be able to show that it is politically cohesive. If the minority group is not politically cohesive, it cannot be said that the selection of a multimember electoral structure thwarts distinctive minority group interests.... Third, the minority must be able to demonstrate that the white majority votes sufficiently as a bloc to enable it—in the absence of special circumstances, such as the minority candidate running unopposed ... usually to defeat the minority's preferred candidate.[43]

Gingles thus placed a great deal of pressure on the states. If a minority group demonstrated that a state failed to draw a majority-minority district where one *could* have been drawn, it could file a section 2 suit under the VRA, claiming that its voting power had been diluted.

Gingles expanded the scope of the franchise from a simple individually-focused right to cast a ballot to include a collective right to a fair representation opportunity. *Gingles*, along with *Allen*, therefore "moved" the American concept of the franchise closer to the Canadian vision that informed the *Saskatchewan Reference*. This, however, created a new dilemma for the American Court.

Since *Gingles* compelled states to accommodate minority voters' demands for majority-minority voting districts and *Reynolds*, *Lucas*, etc., required them to adhere at least somewhat closely to the one-person-one-vote requirement, states had to draw bizarrely shaped districts because minority voters were not always located in geographically compact areas. This evolution of its case law cornered the American Court.

Unlike section 15 of the Charter, the equal protection clause of the American Constitution made no exception for benign discrimination intended to help minorities. Thus, in the American constitutional context, if gerrymandering minority groups out of power was unconstitutional, gerrymandering them *into* power was also constitutionally suspect. This resulted in a new set of voting rights challenges that commenced with *Shaw v. Reno* in 1993.

Shaw v. Reno and the Tension between Individual and Group Voting Rights

In *Shaw v. Reno*, the Supreme Court ruled that a redistricting scheme "unexplainable" on grounds other than race would violate the equal protection clause of the Fourteenth Amendment. Asserting that "reapportionment is one area in which appearances do matter,"[44] the Court argued that if a district had a particularly bizarre shape, it would invite further scrutiny to see whether it had been drawn consciously to enhance the representational opportunities of minority voters. If the record indicated that racial considerations had played a determinative role in the construction of a challenged district and if the district's shape indicated that the legislature had forsaken "traditional districting principles" to such an extent that its outline was "highly irregular," "bizarre," and "irrational on its face," then, the Court argued, the redistricting plan would run afoul of the equal protection clause.[45]

In *Shaw*, the Court acknowledged that the individual right to cast a meaningful vote in a truly competitive political contest—as opposed to casting merely a symbolic vote within a political process that was designed to ensure (or at least enhance the likelihood of) particular outcomes—was now at stake. This aspect of *Shaw* generalized the principle of racial fairness on which the case was grounded: If the districting process should not be gerrymandered to enhance a particular *racial* outcome, on what grounds could it be gerrymandered to enhance *any* particular outcome? In either case, the outcome of the electoral process would, to at least some extent, be foreordained.

In declaring that the creation of bizarrely shaped majority-minority voting districts may be unconstitutional, the Court in *Shaw* essentially reiterated the principle first set forth in 1958 in *Gomillion v. Lightfoot*.[46] There, the Court had ruled that the transformation of Tuskegee, Alabama, into an "uncouth"

23-sided figure designed to disenfranchise Black voters was unconstitutional. Consistency therefore dictated that districts such as the North Carolina 12th congressional district (which gave rise to *Shaw*) had to be unconstitutional as well—unless the constitutional analysis was based on a qualitative distinction between a gerrymanderer's victims.

The Anti-Gerrymandering Principle[47]

In his dissenting opinion in *Shaw*, Justice John Paul Stevens tried to distinguish between the scenarios in *Gomillion* and *Shaw*. He argued that there was a difference between an attempt by a majority to gerrymander a minority out of power and the attempt by the same majority to assist a minority by enhancing the latter's power.

> I believe that the Equal Protection Clause is violated when the State creates the kind of uncouth district boundaries seen in this case, for the sole purpose of making it more difficult for members of a minority group to win an election. The duty to govern impartially is abused when a group with power over the electoral process defines electoral boundaries solely to enhance its own political strength at the expense of any weaker group. That duty, however, is not violated when the majority acts to facilitate the election of a member of a group that lacks such power because it remains under-represented in the state legislature—whether that group is defined by political affiliation, by common economic interests, or by religious, ethnic, or racial characteristics.[48]

Also in dissent, Justice Byron White said that "the question in gerrymandering cases is whether a particular group has been unconstitutionally denied its chance to effectively influence the political process." Thus, an equal protection violation may be found only where the electoral system "*substantially disadvantages certain voters in their opportunity to influence the political process effectively*" (emphasis in original).[49] Since White and Stevens did not believe that the creation of majority-minority districts disadvantaged white voters in North Carolina, they saw no constitutional basis for challenging the districting scheme.

Could remedial redistricting be reconciled with the notion of an unbiased political process? In saying "no," the majority in *Shaw* seemed to make sense in comparing remedial redistricting to "political apartheid" and the racial segregation of school children.[50] If it was impermissible to use race in one, how could it be permissible to do so in the other?

To resolve the dilemma presented in *Shaw*, the Court had to resolve a tension concerning its view of the equal protection clause. Since 1978, when the Court rendered its controversial decision in *Regents of the University of California v. Bakke*,[51] two rival visions of equal protection had informed the Court's jurisprudence concerning racial equality. In *Bakke*, the Court ruled that race, like musical talent, speed in the 100-yard dash, or Slovenian citizenship, could be factored into a public university's admissions decision (and, by extension, other aspects of government policy). By contrast, the Court declared in *Adarand Constructors v. Pena* (1995) that any use of race in public policy should trigger the Court's strict scrutiny.[52] In *Shaw*, the Court majority anticipated the *Adarand* vision of equal protection and struck down the majority-minority districts.

Applying this interpretation of the Fourteenth Amendment to redistricting was a questionable logical exercise. Throughout American history, districts have been drawn to benefit all sorts of ethnic or economic interests. In this respect, then, redistricting has been no more or less plagued by interest group politics than any other aspect of American public policy. To rule that racial preferences were an exception to this tradition required a reading of the equal protection clause that was indeed bizarre and suggested that catering and giving preference to discrete interests was constitutional unless the interests involved were racially defined.[53] Such a reading of the Fourteenth Amendment would render it useless to the racial minority groups it was intended to benefit. The *Bakke* reading of the Fourteenth Amendment conforms more closely to the Madisonian vision of pluralism, makes more logical sense, and avoids the questionable reasoning that informs attempts to declare the use of race (as opposed to other partisan considerations) uniquely unconstitutional.

Supporters of remedial redistricting, such as Stevens, regard the practice as simply ensuring that the so-called fair workings of the political marketplace do not unfairly shut particular minority groups out of the political process. However, Stevens failed to see that the logical implications of his support for remedial gerrymanderers would also justify other attempts to manipulate electoral outcomes.

Daniel Polsby and Karl Popper did. The decision in *Shaw*, they noted, addressed a fundamental problem of representative democracy: "namely, how far a legislature may go in controlling who is elected to it."[54] Whereas Justice Stevens could justify the conscious attempt by a majority to condition electoral results in favour of a minority, Polsby and Popper's reading of *Shaw* asserted that benevolent gerrymanderers were oxymoronic: "Gerrymandering [and other methods of political "cheating"]—whether racial or partisan ...

are cut from the same cloth. What makes them objectionable is the notion that the legislature has strayed from its proper domain and played too large a role in constituting itself."[55]

Thus, in their analysis of *Shaw*, Polsby and Popper expanded the scope of gerrymandering analysis. Whereas the dissent in *Shaw* focused on the relationship between legislative majorities and minorities, Polsby and Popper regarded gerrymandering in the context of the relationship between the polity and its representatives. If elite representatives could alter the people's voice to produce electoral outcomes that did not reflect the popular will, the democratic process would be perverted.

The Transformation of American Voting Rights Jurisprudence

The tensions in *Shaw* ensured that it would not endure as a useful legal precedent. Gradually, the importance of the intractable issue of district shape was diminished. Whether this was due to the inability of scholars or practitioners to develop a consistently useful measure for distinguishing constitutional from unconstitutional shapes, or the realization that the nation was littered with bizarrely shaped districts of no constitutional remarkability is hard to tell. However, it was clear from the Court's internal disputes concerning district outlines that district shape had quickly become a useless legal standard.

Speaking for the Court in *Miller v. Johnson* (1995), Justice Anthony Kennedy modified *Shaw*. He diminished the importance of district shape and focused instead on the issue of legislative intent that Polsby and Popper had emphasized. Granted, the focus remained on *racially*-motivated intent. Nonetheless, the Court now began to discuss whether and how racial concerns could be subsumed by other considerations of electoral design.

> The plaintiff's burden is to show ... that race was the predominant factor motivating the legislature's decision to place a significant number of voters within or without a particular district.... [A] plaintiff must prove that the legislature subordinated traditional race-neutral districting principles, including but not limited to compactness, contiguity, respect for political subdivisions or communities defined by actual shared interests, to racial considerations. Where these or other race-neutral considerations are the basis for redistricting legislation, and are not subordinated to race, a State can "defeat a claim that a district has been gerrymandered on racial lines."[56]

In *Bush v. Vera* (1996), the Court focused again on the intent of the legislature and whether it had merely considered race in the districting process, or whether it had, instead, allowed race to predominate its delibera-tions.[57] The Court discussed whether the existence of a plausible nonracial alternative explanation would protect a challenged districting scheme from constitutional challenge.

The Court wavered. Writing for the Court, Justice Sandra Day O'Connor stated that "[i]f district lines merely correlate with race because they are drawn on the basis of political affiliation, which correlates with race, there is no racial classification to justify."[58]

> The present case is a mixed motive case. The appellants concede that one of Texas' goals in creating the three districts at issue was to produce majority-minority districts, but they also cite evidence that other goals, particularly incumbency protection (including protection of "functional incumbents," i.e., sitting members of the Texas Legislature who had declared an intention to run for open congressional seats), also played a role in the drawing of the district lines. The record does not reflect a history of "'*purely* race-based'" districting revisions.[59]

While the dissenting and other concurring justices in *Bush v. Vera* indicated that the Court was not of one mind regarding O'Connor's view, her opinion laid the basis for the Court's subsumption of race as one of many factors that affect a districting plan. This defused the racial issue that had been the focus of debate since *Gingles*, but it still did not address Polsby and Popper's criticism.

Defusing the Racial Question ...

The Court accepted a state's assertion that its congressional districts were the product of a multitude of factors (only one of which was race) in *Easley v. Cromartie* (2001).[60] Insofar as race did not predominate in the line-draw-ing process, the Court was able to sustain the constitutionality of bizarrely shaped majority-minority districts. The Court ruled that so long as states could demonstrate that some other factor besides race played an important role in the drafting of legislative district lines, the states could defend a districting scheme by explaining that race did not "predominate." As the Court noted:

> In a case such as this one where majority-minority districts (or the approxi-mate equivalent) are at issue and where racial identification correlates highly with political affiliation, the party attacking the legislatively drawn

boundaries must show at the least that the legislature could have achieved its legitimate political objectives in alternative ways that are comparably consistent with traditional districting principles. That party must also show that those districting alternatives would have brought about significantly greater racial balance.[61]

The Court thus drew upon the statement by O'Connor in *Vera*, quoted above.

Supporting North Carolina's assertion that race was only one of several factors (including incumbent protection and partisan balance) that entered into the line-drawing process, the Court stated that "the Constitution does not place an *affirmative* obligation upon the legislature to avoid creating districts that turn out to be heavily, even majority, minority. It simply imposes an obligation not to create such districts for predominantly racial, as opposed to political or traditional, districting motivations."[62]

Easley allowed courts to look at a racially remedial gerrymanderer and declare it nothing more than a partisan or incumbent one. By declaring that race had to be the *predominant* factor in a redistricting plan for it to be unconstitutional, the Court allowed states to defend their plans by offering a plausible partisan alternative explanation for their districting decisions. In this respect, the states could cloak a racial gerrymanderer in partisan clothing and move on.

Conclusion: The Threat to a Meaningful Vote?

The American Court's voting rights and gerrymandering case law now compare to the *Saskatchewan Reference*. It simply took a longer time for the American Court to develop the law to a point at which, like its Canadian counterpart, it could accommodate group and individual aspects of the voting right. One person, one vote is the base principle from which both courts have developed their jurisprudence. For lack of a better term, the American Court has also established a second "anti-gerrymandering" principle that forbids any extraordinary attempt to ensure particular political outcomes.

As long as someone has the power to decide how the electoral process will be organized, there will always be a basis for someone else to assert that the process is biased. The two nations have focused on different aspects of this tension. Since the Canadian Court has not enshrined "rep by pop" in the same way that the American Court has, Canadian observers have occasionally expressed fears about the possibility of minority rule evolving from an attempt to enhance minority representation.[63] By contrast, the one-person-one-vote rule in the United States militates against the possibility of minority rule.

Polsby and Popper demonstrated that while there is a cost to adhering to strict individual voting equality, there is also an equally clear—if not more sinister—cost to allowing the legislature to deviate from it—even in the name of enhancing minority representation. Their statement of the anti-gerrymandering principle put both sides of the minority voting rights debate on the defensive. While some voters may benefit from gerrymandering at the expense of others, and while remedial gerrymandering may alleviate disparities of political influence, Polsby and Popper showed that deferring to legislative controls over the electoral process threatens the electorate's control over the legislature. Once incumbent political actors have the power to manipulate the process by which they are returned to office, they can "lock up" the electoral process by erecting barriers to entry (such as discriminatory ballot access laws, gerrymandered political districts, poll taxes, literacy tests, and so forth). This not only perverts the democratic process, it insulates incumbents from electoral accountability and renders the franchise less meaningful.

More important, the possibility that the legislature may engage in this cartel-like behaviour has engendered skepticism in both courts. It undermines an important premise underpinning calls for judicial modesty when engaging the legislature in a constitutional dialogue. If there is a possibility that a challenged law embodies a "lockup," the Court cannot justify deferring to the legislature or, in the spirit of the dialogue, giving the legislature the last word. Instead, the Court must play a more active role in scrutinizing electoral legislation. This becomes even clearer in the next chapter where we discuss the two supreme courts' decisions concerning political spending and speech.

Notes

1 *Reference re Provincial Electoral Boundaries (Sask.)*, [1991] 2 S.C.R. 158. Hereinafter cited as the *Saskatchewan Reference*.

2 *Baker v. Carr*, 369 U.S. 186 (1962); *Reynolds v. Sims*, 377 U.S. 533 (1964).

3 *Reynolds v. Sims*, 562–63.

4 *Saskatchewan Reference*, 184, 185.

5 Ibid., 183.

6 Ibid., 184.

7 See, e.g., Lani Guinier, *The Tyranny of the Majority* (New York: The Free Press, 1994), 7–10; Pamela Karlan, "The Rights to Vote: Some Pessimism about Formalism," *Texas Law Review* 71 (1993): 1705–40.

8   See generally, Abigail M. Thernstrom, *Whose Votes Count?* (Cambridge: Harvard University Press, 1987); Mark Rush, "The Voting Rights Act and its Discontents," in *The Voting Rights Act: Securing the Ballot*, ed. Richard Valelley (Washington, DC: Congressional Quarterly Press, 2006).

9   Such issues actually arise in our discussion of *Vriend v. Alberta* in Chapter 5 of this book.

10 *Lucas v. Forty-Fourth General Assembly of Colorado*, 377 U.S. 713 (1964).

11 *Allen v. State Board of Elections*, 393 U.S. 544 (1969).

12 See Chandler Davidson and Bernard Grofman, eds., *Quiet Revolution in the South: The Impact of the Voting Rights Act, 1965–1990* (Princeton, NJ: Princeton University Press, 1994).

13 42 U.S.C. 73. Section 2 provides that:

No voting qualification or prerequisite to voting or standard, practice or procedure shall be imposed or applied by any State or political subdivision in a manner which results in a denial or abridgement of the right of any citizen of the United States to vote on account of race or color ... as provided in subsection (b) of this section.

A violation of subsection (a) of this section is established if, based on the totality of circumstances, it is shown that the political processes leading to nomination or election in the State or political subdivision are not equally open to participation by members of a class of citizens ... in that its members have less opportunity than other members of the electorate to participate in the political process and to elect representatives of their choice.... Provided that nothing in this section establishes a right to have members of the protected class elected in numbers equal to their proportion in the population.

14 See, e.g., Andrew Sancton, "Eroding Representation by Population in the Canadian House of Commons: The *Representation Act*, 1985," *Canadian Journal of Political Science* 23 (September 1992): 441–57; Russell Alan Williams, "Comparing Federal Electoral Redistributions: Straining Canada's System of Representation" (paper presented at the Annual Meeting of the Canadian Political Science Association, Quebec City, June 2001).

15 See generally, John C. Courtney, Peter MacKinnon, and David E. Smith, eds., *Drawing Boundaries: Legislatures, Courts, and Electoral Values* (Saskatoon: Fifth House, 1992).

16 *Shaw v. Reno*, 509 U.S. 630 (1993).

17 *Colegrove v. Green*, 381 U.S. 549 (1946).

18 Ibid., 566.

19 Ibid.

20 Ibid., 571.

21 *Baker v. Carr*, 197–98.

22 Ibid., 319.

23 *Reynolds v. Sims*, 377 U.S. 533 (1964).

24 Ibid., 579–80.

25 *Lucas v. Forty-Fourth General Assembly of Colorado*, 736–37.

26 John Hart Ely, *Democracy and Distrust* (Cambridge: Harvard University Press, 1980), 124.

27 Samuel Issacharoff and Richard Pildes, "Politics As Markets: Partisan Lockups of the Democratic Process," *Stanford Law Review* 50 (1998): 643–717.

28 See generally, Courtney, MacKinnon, and Smith, *Drawing Boundaries*. See also Sancton, "Eroding Representation"; Russell Alan Williams, "The 279 Formula: and Federal Redistributions: Canada's System of Representation in Crisis," *Annual Review of Canadian Studies* 35 (2005): 99–134; Richard W. Jenkins, "Untangling the Politics of Electoral Boundaries in Canada, 1993–1997," *The American Review of Canadian Studies* 28 (1998): 517–38.

29 For an exhaustive discussion of Canadian, American, and Australian redistricting law, see Elizabeth Daly, "Idealists, Pragmatists and Textualists: Judging Electoral Districts in America, Canada and Australia," *Boston College International & Comparative Law Review* 21 (1998): 261–383.

30 *Reference re Provincial Electoral Boundaries*, 90 Sask. R. 174, 186 (1991).

31 *Saskatchewan Reference*, 183.

32 Ibid., 185.

33 Ibid., 184.

34 *Dixon v. British Columbia*, 59 D.L.R. (4th) 247 (1989).

35 *Saskatchewan Reference*, 185.

36 Ibid., 171.

37 Ibid., 174, Cory, et. al., dissenting.

38 See, e.g., *U.S. Department of Commerce v. Montana*, 502 U.S. 442 (1992).

39 *Karcher v. Daggett*, 462 U.S. 725 (1983).

40 More recently, the Court stated that it would tolerate population deviations among state legislative districts of up to 5 per cent (*Voinovich v. Quilter*, 507 U.S. 146 [1993]). The Court has not offered a clear explanation for the difference in its approach to congressional and state legislative redistricting. In *Karcher* (732–33), it stated that there could be no justification for local interests interfering with the franchise at the congressional level. However, at the local level, local concerns clearly played a more significant role in drawing legislative district maps:

[A]bsolute population equality [must] be the paramount objective of apportionment only in the case of congressional districts, for which the command of Article I, [Section] 2 as regards the National Legislature outweighs the local interests that a State may deem relevant in apportioning districts for representatives to state and local legislatures, but we have not questioned the population equality standard for congressional districts.

41 *Allen v. State Board of Elections*, 565–66, internal citations omitted.

42 *Thornburg v. Gingles*, 478 U.S. 30 (1986).

43 *Thornburg v. Gingles*, 50–51, internal citations omitted.

44 *Shaw v. Reno*, 509 U.S. 630 at 647.

45 Ibid., 648.

46 *Gomillion v. Lightfoot*, 364 U.S. 339 (1958).

47   See Daniel D. Polsby and Robert D. Popper, "Ugly: An Inquiry into the Problem of Racial Gerrymandering under the Voting Rights Act," *Michigan Law Review* 92 (1993): 652–82.

48   *Shaw v. Reno*, 677, Stevens, J., dissenting.

49   Ibid., 653.

50   Ibid., 647.

51   *Regents of the University of California v. Bakke*, 438 U.S. 912 (1978).

52   *Adarand Constructors v. Pena*, 515 U.S. 200 (1995). For a thoughtful summary and assessment of this strain in equal protection jurisprudence see T. Alexander Aleinikoff and Samuel Issacharoff, "Race and Redistricting: Drawing Lines after *Shaw v. Reno*," *Michigan Law Review* 92 (1993): 588, 592–603.

53   This view is reflected in Justice Thomas's opinions in *Grutter v. Bollinger* (123 S. Ct. 2325 [2003]) and *Gratz v. Bollinger* (123 S. Ct. 2411 [2003]). He regards affirmative action on the basis of race as "discrimination" (see *Grutter*, 2350). However, according to Thomas, other forms of preference—such as political patronage and hiring and firing—are constitutional because they "do not violate any explicit text of the Constitution" and "have been regarded as constitutional ever since the framing." See *Board of County Commissioners, Wabansee County, Kansas v. Umbehr*, 516 U.S. 668 at 687 (1996), Scalia and Thomas dissenting.

54   Polsby and Popper, "The Problem of Racial Gerrymandering," 654.

55   Ibid., 676.

56   *Miller v. Johnson*, 515 U.S. 900 at 916 (1995).

57   *Bush v. Vera*, 517 U.S. 952 (1996).

58   Ibid., 968.

59   Ibid., 959.

60   *Easley v. Cromartie*, 532 U.S. 234 (2001).

61   *Easley v. Cromartie*, 258.

62   *Easley v. Cromartie*, 248.

63   See endnote 14 above.

chapter four

A Tale of Two Campaign Spending Decisions[1]

The decisions concerning prisoners' voting rights discussed in Chapter 2 demonstrate important differences in how the two supreme courts regard access to and the scope of the franchise, as well as their role with respect to the elected branches of government. Nonetheless, these decisions also demonstrate how much the two courts have in common. The case law concerning the scope and definition of the franchise and redistribution confirms how much Canadian and American law have converged despite assertions that the jurisprudential traditions of both countries are quite different. In this chapter, we document a similar convergence in the two courts' campaign spending decisions.

As we noted in the Introduction, this book was inspired by the similarities in the campaign spending decisions by the two courts in *Harper v. Canada* and *McConnell v. Federal Election Commission*. The common terms of debate within the two courts were especially striking to us because they arose within the context of a scholarly consensus about the stark differences in the two courts' theories of rights and democracy. Canadian critics such as Colin Feasby, Heather MacIvor, and Janet Hiebert have asserted that the two nations' campaign spending decisions were rooted in fundamentally different conceptions of individual rights and theories of democracy and political equality. We respectfully disagree with this assessment.

Canadian analysts of campaign spending decisions in both nations have cast the Canadian Court's decisions in opposition to a talismanic American decision, *Buckley v. Valeo* (1974).[2] In *Buckley*, the American Supreme Court struck down key amendments made in 1974 to the Federal Election Campaign Act (FECA) of 1971. As amended, FECA placed restrictions on the amount of money that individuals or political action committees could contribute toward or spend on behalf of parties or candidates. As well, it restricted the amount of money that parties could contribute toward or spend in support of their own nominees.

Buckley, however, was decided in 1974. The American Supreme Court has rendered many subsequent campaign spending decisions that qualify *Buckley* and, we argue, manifest an evolution in the Court's thinking. As a result, it is inaccurate to rely on *Buckley* to characterize American campaign spending law. Instead, a broader look at the evolution of the US Court's campaign spending decisions demonstrates that the American justices have engaged in a debate about the scope and definition of democratic rights that compares, again, to that which has occurred within the Canadian Supreme Court. Furthermore, we demonstrate that after *Harper* and *McConnell*, both courts now have remarkably similar views about the rights at stake in campaign spending controversies.

We turn now to discuss *Buckley* and how it has been read too narrowly by Canadian scholars and how they have therefore overstated the differences between the American and Canadian courts' approaches to campaign spending. The common evolution that we observe has also led to the development of a growing concern in both courts that challenges to election laws expose an important conflict of interest on the part of the legislature. Insofar as electoral regulations govern the process by which the legislature is reconstituted, elected officials stand to benefit from any laws that might insulate them from political competition.

A growing number of justices on both courts now share this skepticism about the motives behind electoral regulation. We suggest that this aspect of the convergence between the two courts has especially important implications for the Canadian Supreme Court because it undermines two important premises on which the dialogic vision of constitutional interpretation is grounded: mutual respect between the judiciary and the rest of the government, and judicial willingness to defer to the legislature based on a trust of the latter's motives.

Buckley v. Valeo: Another Straw Figure?

An important aspect of *Buckley* was the Court's distinction between restrictions on *contributions* to political parties or candidates and *independent spending* by groups or individuals on behalf of, in support of, or against particular candidates or parties. Whereas, the Court noted, contribution limits clearly militated against corruption and the appearance thereof by limiting the extent to which contributors could seek to garner quid pro quo political favours, spending by third parties or candidates presented no such quid pro quo opportunities and, therefore, limits to such spending could not be sustained. These restrictions had been challenged because plaintiffs regarded them as infringements on political speech.

The Supreme Court concluded that restrictions on contributions were constitutional because their infringement on political expression was minimal. As well, Congress's desire to prevent corruption, or at least remove the appearance thereof, outweighed the minimal impairment caused by contribution limits on political expression.

A contribution serves as a general expression of support for the candidate and his views, but does not communicate the underlying basis for the support. The quantity of communication by the contributor does not increase perceptibly with the size of the contribution, since the expression rests solely on the undifferentiated, symbolic act of contributing. At most, the size of the contribution provides a very rough index of the intensity of the contributor's support for the candidate. A limitation on the amount of money a person may give to a candidate or campaign organization thus involves little direct restraint on his political communication, for it permits the symbolic expression of support evidenced by a contribution but does not in any way infringe the contributor's freedom to discuss candidates and issues.[3]

The Court regarded restrictions on spending in a different light. "Independent" spending[4] by individuals during an election campaign entailed exercising this same "freedom to discuss candidates and issues." Whereas contributions to a particular candidate may create the appearance of a quid pro quo exchange of influence between the candidate and the contributor, the expression of a political opinion (and spending the money to express it effectively) by an individual did not comprise the same quid pro quo opportunity.

The Court's concerns about corruption were therefore somewhat complex. On the one hand, it understood and supported efforts to prevent the unfair promotion of influence peddling. This constituted a violation of the rules of the political marketplace that might be compared to the use and dissemination of "insider information" in the financial marketplace.

However, the American Court asserted that the political marketplace should be as open and free as possible so that the conveyance and exchange of political opinion could be maximized. The Court's concern about the openness of the political marketplace was manifested in its analysis of the threat that independent spending restrictions posed to the ability of citizens and interest groups to associate (and combine financial resources) for the advocacy of particular interests.

> [T]he independent expenditure ceiling ... fails to serve any substantial governmental interest in stemming the reality or appearance of corruption in the electoral process, it heavily burdens core First Amendment expression. For the First Amendment right to speak one's mind ... includes the right to engage in "'vigorous advocacy' no less than 'abstract discussion'".... Advocacy of the election or defeat of candidates for federal office is no less entitled to protection under the First Amendment than the discussion of political policy generally or advocacy of the passage or defeat of legislation.[5]

The Court thus concluded that restrictions on independent spending qua political speech had to be based on a compelling justification. Insofar as Congress had stated only the desire to control corruption (defined essentially as quid pro quo exchange of influence) as a basis for controlling spending, the Court saw no clear connection between using one's financial resources to state or broadcast an opinion and corruption of the political process, so defined. It therefore struck down the spending restrictions.

Canadian critics regard *Buckley* as a narrow decision predicated on the unyielding protection of individual speech rights at the expense of political equality and a more robust political process.[6] We disagree. If anything, the American Court has constantly sought to balance its desire to defer to the authority of the Congress with its goal of protecting the integrity of the political marketplace. In an especially revealing footnote, for example, the Court noted: "Democracy depends on a well-informed electorate, not a citizenry legislatively limited in its ability to discuss and debate candidates and issues."[7]

There may be more than one way to promote the civic capacity of the polity. The Court wanted Congress to demonstrate that it had sufficient evidence to prove that restricting the right to engage in political speech would enhance the democratic process. In an important passage for our purposes (and for those of critics who seek to distinguish American and Canadian jurisprudence), the Court said that Congress's desire to level the political playing field was insufficient to justify dampening political discussion by restricting political spending.

> It is argued, however, that the ancillary governmental interest in equalizing the relative ability of individuals and groups to influence the outcome of elections serves to justify the limitation on express advocacy of the election or defeat of candidates.... But the concept that government may restrict the speech of some elements of our society in order to enhance the relative voice of others is wholly foreign to the First Amendment, which was designed to secure the widest possible dissemination of information from diverse and antagonistic sources, and to assure unfettered interchange of ideas for the bringing about of political and social changes desired by the people. The First Amendment's protection against governmental abridgment of free expression cannot properly be made to depend on a person's financial ability to engage in public discussion.[8]

Thus, the American Court argued that the equalization of speech and influence was not a valid constitutional end in itself. Nonetheless, it did not contend that individuals had an unfettered right to speak. Instead, the Court regarded the *individual* speech right as a vital *instrument* for the promotion of a more robust democracy. Insofar as the congressional desire to equalize (or, at least, diminish the inequality of) political influence was not grounded on any reference to limiting quid pro quo corruption, nor was it based in terms of enhancing the collective quality of democratic deliberation, the Court saw no reason to sustain this restriction on free speech.[9]

A Different Canadian Vision? The Egalitarian and Libertarian Conception of Democracy in Canada

The American Court's decision in *Buckley* was based on a narrow definition of "corruption": a quid pro quo exchange of influence. It did not regard inequality of political influence brought about by differences in wealth or political prowess as a "corruption" of the political marketplace.

Canadian critics of *Buckley* use a broader definition of corruption. In promoting campaign spending restrictions, Patrick Monahan argued that a political system in which disparities in wealth not only enhance one's capacity to speak but also one's ability to attain political success needed regulation. He did not refer specifically to this situation as one that is "corrupt," but he nevertheless regarded it as a corruption of the democratic process. In his view, campaign spending restrictions are "designed to ensure that no one political perspective is permitted to drown out the competing messages in the electoral marketplace."[10]

While Monahan was among the first to suggest that the Charter embodied an egalitarian spirit, scholars such as Colin Feasby and Heather MacIvor have argued more recently that the Supreme Court of Canada's "egalitarian" approach to constitutional questions concerning the electoral process is antithetical to what they regard as being the US Court's libertarian vision.[11] We believe that this conclusion is too narrow. *Buckley* cannot be categorized simply as "libertarian" and it is inaccurate to suggest that the rest of the US Court's campaign spending decisions fit neatly into this description. Similarly, our following analysis of the three cases comprising Canada's "egalitarian" model (*Libman*, *Figueroa*, and *Harper*) also indicates that they are too complex to fit neatly into one "egalitarian" category.

Background: The Egalitarian Model in the Canadian Court

Feasby and MacIvor draw upon Frederick Schauer's development of the egalitarian-libertarian distinction in his article, "Judicial Review of the Devices of Democracy." Under the egalitarian model, "a state of affairs in which some voices may be more influential than others, or have more power in fact to produce political outcomes than others, is suspect."[12] In contrast, the libertarian model "stresses the liberty dimension of democracy more than the equality dimension" and is "more skeptical of attempts to limit individual, organizational or corporate use of wealth in political campaigns."[13]

While Schauer cast his discussion in terms of how American campaign finance jurisprudence had wrestled with these two competing conceptions of democracy, Feasby explained that the American Court's campaign spending decisions represent "almost a complete triumph" of the libertarian vision:

> *Buckley* endorses the libertarian view that free speech is the pre-eminent concern in a democratic society and allows only the limitation of speech where corruption is a demonstrable risk. This has had the unfortunate result of precluding meaningful containment of the cost of the American

democratic process and has contributed to the recent controversies over campaign fundraising.[14]

He therefore concluded that *Buckley* stands for the proposition that "equality is an irrelevant consideration in the limitation of political speech" and that "in the United States, the only justifiable restrictions of political speech are those that go to the heart of the electoral process—namely, corruption."[15]

The theoretical differences between the two visions of democracy are stark. The libertarian model promotes a laissez-faire approach to regulation of the political marketplace of ideas. Feasby says that this deleteriously affects political equality and the overall integrity and quality of the democratic process: "The libertarian conception eschews State controls and permits those with greater resources or abilities to express themselves disproportionately in the so-called 'marketplace of ideas.'"[16] In contrast, "the egalitarian conception of democracy is an extension of the 'one person-one vote' principle which stands for the proposition that each person's voice in the democratic process is of equal worth."[17] Under the egalitarian approach, speech in a democracy

is analogous to other institutional forms of political expression where, in order for there to be effective deliberation, it is necessary that there be regulation of expression to some degree. Implicit in such a view is that some speakers and some subjects are more important or relevant than others and should be given priority.[18]

Feasby explains that the egalitarian approach to democracy depends on active state regulation and administration of the democratic process. This entails regulating the speech of some individuals in favour or in support of others. Drawing upon the work of Cass Sunstein and Owen Fiss, Feasby summarizes the basic principles of the egalitarian vision of democracy:

1. equality of liberty is more important than absolute liberty;
2. equality of liberty may only be achieved by limiting freedoms of the wealthy;
3. this may only be achieved through State action.

He then explains that these premises lead to the following conclusion:

[In some situations] the state may have to act to further the robustness of public debate in circumstances where powers outside the state are stifling speech. It may have to allocate public resources—hand out megaphones—to those whose voices would not otherwise be heard in the public square. It may even have to silence the voices of some in order to hear the voices of the others. Sometimes there is simply no other way.[19]

By contrast, in the libertarian vision, "the citizen as voter has a right to uncontrolled access to information."[20] According to the libertarian model,

[a]ny manipulation of the flow of information affects the ability of the electorate to be sovereign. This is encapsulated by the United States Supreme Court in *Buckley*: "In the free society ordained by our Constitution it is not the government, but the people—individually as citizens and candidates and collectively as associations and political committees—who must retain control over the quantity and range of debate on public issues in a political campaign." Central to this conception of electoral regulation is distrust of the government to set rules for the election of future governments.[21]

In essence, the libertarian model calls for virtually no regulation of the political marketplace of ideas. It is based on a distrust of the government and a belief that individuals will, through their self-interested behaviour, combine to form a fair and effective political marketplace free of government interference.

There is no gainsaying that *Buckley*, along with other aspects of the American political process, such as the direct primary, gave rise to a host of practices that have indeed made American campaigns more expensive and correspondingly farther out of reach for the poor or middle class. Nonetheless, while interest groups may have taken advantage of the loopholes in *Buckley*, this does not signify that the US Supreme Court dismissed the importance of inequalities in wealth or the sincerity of Congress's desire to constrain them. Inequality of political influence that arises from disparities in wealth was simply not a component of the Court's definition of corruption—at first. However, as we discuss below, the development of the American Supreme Court's campaign finance decisions after *Buckley* belies the assertion that it has no appreciation for the distorting influence of disparities in wealth. In fact, the American Court's jurisprudence since *Buckley* indicates that it is committed to balancing both the libertarian and egalitarian impulses that Feasby describes.

The Development of the Egalitarian Model in the Canadian Court

Feasby argued that the Canadian Court developed an egalitarian theory of politics in the course of three cases: *Libman v. Quebec* (1997), *Figueroa v. Canada* (2003), and *Harper v. Canada* (2006). *Libman* entailed a challenge to Quebec's decision to hold a referendum on a set of proposed amendments to the Canadian Constitution (the Charlottetown Accord) under the auspices of the provincial Referendum Act instead of under the federal law. Quebec organized two "umbrella committees" in favour of and against the accord. The Referendum Act allowed only these "national" committees, or the groups affiliated with them, to incur "regulated expenses" associated with the referendum campaign. Any group wishing to participate in the referendum campaign was, therefore, required to affiliate with either the "oui" or "non" umbrella committees. Robert Libman, leader and founding member of the Anglo-rights Equality Party, advocated abstaining from the referendum vote. However, the act did not allow him to incur regulated expenses unless he affiliated with one of the two committees—thereby undermining his abstentionist position.

The Supreme Court was sympathetic to the goals of the Referendum Act. Acknowledging that it was vital for Quebec to promote the appearance of fairness in the referendum process, the Court stated:

> The basic objective of the Act at issue is to guarantee the democratic nature of referendums by promoting equality between the options submitted by the government and seeking to promote free and informed voting. It provides for control of spending by the national committees during a referendum campaign, as well as control of spending by independent individuals or groups who do not wish to or who cannot join or affiliate themselves with either of the national committees, in order to promote a certain equality of access to media of expression.[22]

Feasby characterizes this is a "classic statement" of the notion of fairness as it had come to be understood in the context of both the Canada Elections Act and the Quebec Referendum Act.[23] The Court went on to explain:

> [T]he objective of the Act is, first, egalitarian in that it is intended to prevent the most affluent members of society from exerting a disproportionate influence by dominating the referendum debate through access to greater resources. What is sought is in a sense an equality of participation and

influence between the proponents of each option. Second, from the voters' point of view, the system is designed to permit an informed choice to be made by ensuring that some positions are not buried by others. Finally, as a related point, the system is designed to preserve the confidence of the electorate in a democratic process that it knows will not be dominated by the power of money.[24]

Despite its supporting the goals of the Quebec Referendum Act, the Court upheld Libman's challenge. While supporting the egalitarian spirit of the act, the Court noted that the manner in which the egalitarian model was imposed in the case ended up restricting the speech rights of those who would not or could not join either side of the debate. Accordingly, the pursuit of systemic political equality imposed too much of an unfair burden on those third parties who did not wish to affiliate with either the "yes" or "no" camps regarding the Charlottetown Accord referendum. As a result, citizens were forced either to align with and support the dissemination of opinions with which they did not or could not agree, or remain silent.

While sympathetic to the goal of balancing political speech and ensuring that both the yes and no camps were able to convey their arguments effectively, the Court explained that limiting voters' options to joining one of two camps limited the *number* of points of view expressed on the referendum—not the *volume* with which they were expressed. Accordingly, the Court could not sustain this particular spending limit, even though it was generally supportive of the goal of ensuring equality:

> [L]imits on spending by third parties in addition to the limits imposed on the national committees are necessary and must be far stricter than those on spending by the national committees in order to ensure that the system of limits and a balance in resources is effective. Nonetheless, we are of the view that the limits imposed ... cannot meet the minimal impairment test in the case of individuals and groups who can neither join the national committees nor participate in the affiliation system.[25]

It is important to note that in this case the Court cast equality in instrumental terms: Equality was not an end in itself. Instead, equality among speakers and spenders must result in the dissemination of more points of view in the political marketplace and, therefore, an improved democratic process in which better educated, more informed voters participate and exchange views.

Libman can therefore be regarded at best as a qualified endorsement of the egalitarian vision. Insofar as the decision rectified the unequal treatment afforded the abstentionists, it is unquestionably egalitarian. But the ruling also demonstrates a distrust of government attempts to control or channel political debate—even in the name of political equality. In this respect, equality is not an end in itself. Rather, it is a means to ensuring a better democratic process and the opportunity to cast a meaningful vote (or not to vote at all, as Libman advocated).

Figueroa v. Canada

In *Figueroa v. Canada*, the Court ruled that sections 24(2), 24(3), and 28(2) of the Canada Elections Act were an unconstitutional infringement of the right to vote contained in section 3 of the Charter.[26] The government justified the restriction by arguing that it wished to preserve the integrity of the political finance regime by preventing the creation of fictional or fraudulent political parties and to promote the representativeness of the electoral process by fostering the creation of broad-based political parties.[27]

MacIvor[28] and Feasby[29] both suggest that *Figueroa* also embodied the egalitarian theory of politics.[30] It resolved what MacIvor described as a "straightforward clash between the party-equality and two-tier approaches" to laws governing political parties. MacIvor casts *Figueroa* in terms of a debate between libertarians who favoured the two-tier approach to political party rights (which treats large and small parties differently) and egalitarians who did not. The 50-seat threshold was designed in part to promote the formation of majority governments (by using the threshold to discourage the formation of small parties). In striking the threshold down, Feasby says that the Court "held that the [egalitarian] quality of the electoral process is more important than the outcome."[31]

While one can look at the holding in *Figueroa* as an endorsement of the egalitarian position, the decision does not indicate that egalitarianism was the principal emphasis of the Court's decision. Speaking for the Court in *Figueroa*, Justice Frank Iacobucci dismissed the 50-candidate threshold as "viewpoint discrimination" against minor parties and those voters who sought to gain representation by voting for them. For Iacobucci, the right to play a meaningful role in the electoral process entailed the right to have one's political views expressed on equal terms with all other political views. This meant that the state could not act "to hinder or condemn a political view without harming the openness of Canadian democracy."[32]

99

A key aspect of the Court's calculus was the protection of each citizen's right to meaningful participation. Insofar as the threshold made it more difficult for some parties to campaign and therefore made it correspondingly harder for some voters to express themselves on election day, it unconstitutionally infringed upon the "right of each citizen to play a meaningful role in the electoral process."[33] This right was infringed to the extent that laws such as the 50-candidate threshold either (1) limited the choices available to voters on election day, or (2) correspondingly limited the number of viewpoints upon which a voter could draw in making his or her election-day decision. Thus, the right to a meaningful vote was the principal focus of *Figueroa*:

> The right to play a meaningful role in the electoral process includes the right of each citizen to exercise the right to vote in a manner that accurately reflects his or her preferences. In order to exercise the right to vote in this manner, citizens must be able to assess the relative strengths and weaknesses of each party's platform—and in order to assess the relative strengths and weaknesses of each party, voters must have access to information about each candidate. As a consequence, legislation that exacerbates a pre-existing disparity in the capacity of the various political parties to communicate their positions to the general public is inconsistent with s. 3.... By derogating from the capacity of marginal or regional parties to present their ideas and opinions to the general public, it undermines the right of each citizen to information that might influence the manner in which she or he exercises the right to vote.[34]

This passage indicates that while it may be reasonable to regard *Figueroa* as an egalitarian decision, the support for the egalitarian vision is, once again, predicated on its instrumentality in furthering the *individual* right to cast a meaningful vote.[35]

The *Figueroa* majority placed the integrity of the franchise above other values that the government might seek to foster through electoral regulation. Promoting particular types of political parties or seeking to foster the formation of majority governments might be laudable legislative goals. However, if pursuing those goals diminished the integrity or meaningful exercise of the franchise, the legislation would be unconstitutional. The Court made this clear when it restated its understanding of the right to vote laid out in section 3 of the Charter. The Court stated:

[T]he right of each citizen to participate in the political life of the country is one that is of fundamental importance in a free and democratic society and suggests that s. 3 should be interpreted in a manner that ensures that this right of participation embraces a content commensurate with the importance of individual participation in the selection of elected representatives in a free and democratic state. Defining the purpose of s. 3 with reference to the right of each citizen to play a meaningful role in the electoral process, rather than the composition of Parliament subsequent to an election, better ensures that the right of participation that s. 3 explicitly protects is not construed too narrowly.[36]

This suggests that the two-tiered treatment of political parties is not in and of itself unconstitutional. In fact, as MacIvor noted, while registered parties may qualify for reimbursement of 60 per cent of their declared election expenses, in order to do so a party must win 2 per cent of the national vote or 5 per cent of the vote in the constituencies where it runs candidates. As well, parties receive a share of free broadcast air time equal to their proportion of the vote and seat shares from the previous election.[37] Thus, the "two-tiered" system remains in place in Canada. While it is true that *Figueroa* resulted in significant changes to the laws governing political parties, the law still has a disparate impact on political parties. This is constitutional, in the Court's opinion, so long as it does not diminish the impact of the individual right to cast a meaningful vote.

This aspect of the Court's opinion is especially important because the majority challenged Justice Louis LeBel's assertion in dissent that the franchise can and should be balanced against other collective goals. LeBel argued that the majority had taken an excessively individualistic approach to the franchise that overlooked important collective and communitarian aspects of Canadian jurisprudence. Explaining that section 3 is also concerned with the representation of communities, LeBel maintained that balancing individual and communitarian aspects of the franchise "can render participation more meaningful and result in better representation of communities and national political preferences."[38]

LeBel based his argument upon Chief Justice Beverley McLachlin's rejection of the strict equality principle in the *Saskatchewan Reference*. Voter parity, said LeBel, is only one of the factors, "albeit a factor of primary importance," to be taken into account in determining whether effective representation has been provided.[39] In response, Justice Iacobucci explained that while effective representation (or other democratic goals) might justify deviation from strict voter parity, the individual right to cast a meaningful ballot was not subject to infringement. According to Iacobucci, McLachlin's opinion in the *Saskatchewan Reference* did not "indicate that the right of each citizen to play a meaningful role in the electoral process is to be balanced against countervailing values, such as the collective interest in the aggregation of political preferences." Rather, he argued:

> [T]he use of such phrases reflects that the purpose of s. 3 is not to protect the right of each citizen to play an *unlimited* role in the electoral process, but to protect the right of each citizen to play a *meaningful* role in the electoral process; the mere fact that the legislation departs from absolute voter equality or restricts the capacity of a citizen to participate in the electoral process is an insufficient basis on which to conclude that it interferes with the right of each citizen to play a meaningful role in the electoral process. But if the legislation does, in fact, interfere with the capacity of each citizen to play a meaningful role in the electoral process, it is inconsistent with s. 3. Any corresponding benefits related to democratic values other than the right of each citizen to play a meaningful role must be considered under s. 1 (emphasis in original).[40]

Here, then, a majority of the Court clearly qualifies its support of the egalitarian vision and the role the state may play in fostering it. Whereas Feasby suggested that *Libman* and *Figueroa* (and later, *Harper*) manifest the Supreme Court's shift toward the egalitarian model of judicial review,[41] the above passage clearly suggests that the protection of the meaningful vote takes precedence over the promotion of egalitarianism. It also manifests a judicial refusal to defer to legislative balancing or to give the legislature the benefit of the doubt or the last word when it comes to setting electoral regulations. Thus, the Court did not reject egalitarianism in favour of a libertarian model of the franchise. Instead, it noted that legislatively imposed egalitarianism necessitated judicial scrutiny because it could come at the expense of the *meaningful exercise* of the franchise.

LeBel had reasserted what he believed to be the core holding in the *Saskatchewan Reference*:

> [A]dverse effects on the capacity of an individual citizen to participate are not equivalent, in and of themselves, to a denial of meaningful participation or effective representation. In order to determine whether such measures

conflict with s. 3, their nature must be identified and their impact must be weighed in the full context of the political system.[42]

Accordingly, LeBel argued that the right to "effective representation" enshrined in section 3 did not speak to one particular manner in which to balance individual and collective aspects of voting. Speaking to McLachlin's calculus in the *Saskatchewan Reference*, LeBel continued:

> This Court recognized in the *Saskatchewan Reference* that some diminution of one aspect of effective representation (parity) can ultimately result in the provision of more effective representation. This acknowledgement suggests that effective representation is not reducible to any single value, but consists of many different components. Citizens may make political choices that represent their interests as individuals, or they may attach more importance to being represented as members of communities of interest both narrow and broad. The constitutional obligation to ensure that this complex matrix of interests is represented effectively allows for a fairly wide range of alternatives, each combining or prioritizing the various elements at play in a different way. For example, if a province were to design its electoral districts to be as close to numerical equality as practically possible, this arrangement might (depending on the particular facts and context) be just as acceptable in terms of s. 3 as an electoral map designed to enhance the voting power of minority communities.[43]

Thus, LeBel regarded disadvantaged political parties in *Figueroa* in the same light as under-represented voters in the *Saskatchewan Reference*. In both instances, the inequality among individuals (voters or political parties) was justified because it resulted in a better representational scheme.[44] LeBel therefore chastised the Court for focusing on the "strictly individual aspects of participation in the political process"[45] and for imposing one judicially preferred view of better government at the expense of a competing vision of government advocated by Parliament.[46]

The *Figueroa* majority's disagreement with LeBel cannot necessarily be cast in terms of a defence of individualism. *Figueroa* embodies elements of egalitarian and libertarian thinking. But these visions of democracy are ultimately subordinate to the preservation of a meaningful individual right to vote. Of course, restricting some aspects of the individual exercise of the franchise may, in promoting the collective or egalitarian aspects of the franchise, ultimately enhance the meaning of the individual right to vote.

This becomes especially clear in the Court's deliberations about campaign spending restrictions in *Harper*. As we see in *Harper*, the Court again divided concerning the manner in which the government promoted equality. In *Harper*, however, Chief Justice McLachlin dissented—and her reasoning demonstrates that she reconsidered (or at least, reformulated) the analysis on which she based her opinion in the *Saskatchewan Reference*.

Harper v. Canada: Judicial Skepticism on the Rise

Harper v. Canada entailed a challenge to limits placed on third-party spending under the 2000 Canada Elections Act.[47] The key focus of the case dealt with section 350(1) of the act, which limited independent election advertising expenses to no more than $3,000 per constituency and $150,000 nationally. Harper contended that the spending limits were too low and therefore violated the rights to speak and vote set forth in sections 2 and 3 of the Charter.

The Court relied heavily on *Libman* and the *Sasakatchewan Reference* to sustain the spending restrictions. Focusing on the disparate impact that gross differences in wealth could have on the political process, the Court asserted that the egalitarian model is an "essential component of our democratic society." This model, the Court said, "is premised on the notion that individuals should have an equal opportunity to participate in the electoral process."[48]

The Court stated that individual speech could be regulated so that the aggregate volume and diversity of speech could be enhanced. If only a few powerful voices were able to dominate political discourse, the polity and the quality and content of political discourse would suffer. This, in turn, would adversely affect the capacity of individual citizens to participate in the electoral process. Continuing, the Court said:

> The current third party election advertising regime is Parliament's response to this Court's decision in *Libman*. The regime is clearly structured on the egalitarian model of elections. The overarching objective of the regime is to promote electoral fairness by creating equality in the political discourse. The regime promotes the equal dissemination of points of view by limiting the election advertising of third parties who, as this Court has recognized, are important and influential participants in the electoral process. The advancement of equality and fairness in elections ultimately encourages public confidence in the electoral system. Thus, broadly speaking, the third party election advertising regime is consistent with an egalitarian conception of elections and the principles endorsed by this Court in *Libman*.[49]

Thus, the unrestrained exercise of individual speech rights—of groups or voters—was less important than the promotion of a collective speech right. That is, the value of individual rights was based on their instrumentality in promoting the quality of the collective discourse of the polity:

> The overarching objective of the third party election advertising limits is electoral fairness. Equality in the political discourse promotes electoral fairness and is achieved, in part, by restricting the participation of those who have access to significant financial resources. The more voices that have access to the political discourse, the more voters will be empowered to exercise their right in a meaningful and informed manner. Canadians understandably have greater confidence in an electoral system which ultimately encourages increased participation.[50]

Insofar as the franchise embodies a right to effective political participation, *Harper* defines that effectiveness to include diversity of voter voice and information. *Harper* stands for the proposition that voters should have access to broad and diverse sources of information prior to casting their ballots among those same election-day choices. An informed voter is the vital building block of Canadian democracy, and the government should take the steps necessary to preserve the free flow of ideas. To the extent that promoting voter equality also enhances the meaningfulness of the franchise, corresponding restrictions on individual speech rights are in keeping with section 3 of the Charter:

> The question, then, is what promotes an informed voter? For voters to be able to hear all points of view, the information disseminated by third parties, candidates and political parties cannot be unlimited. In the absence of spending limits, it is possible for the affluent or a number of persons or groups pooling their resources and acting in concert to dominate the political discourse.... If a few groups are able to flood the electoral discourse with their message, it is possible, indeed likely, that the voices of some will be drowned out. Where those having access to the most resources monopolize the election discourse, their opponents will be deprived of a reasonable opportunity to speak and be heard. This unequal dissemination of points of view undermines the voter's ability to be adequately informed of all views. In this way, equality in the political discourse is necessary for meaningful participation in the electoral process and ultimately enhances the right to vote.[51]

The Court sustained the challenged sections of the Elections Act because they were designed to promote robust political debate by seeking to increase the number of political voices that could be heard (by reducing the impact of those voices that could drown out others). In contrast, the laws in *Libman* and *Figueroa* had the opposite effect. Thus, the restrictions on speech in *Harper* were justified because they promoted the collective capacity to engage in a meaningful democratic debate.[52] The *number* of voices was not limited (as was the case in *Libman* and *Figueroa*). In fact, by essentially limiting the *volume* with which some overpowering interests might broadcast their message, the Court endorsed the notion that equality could promote diversity and with it, a more meaningful exercise of the franchise. To do this, the state "can provide a voice to those who might otherwise not be heard," or it can "restrict the voices which dominate the political discourse so that others may be heard as well."[53] By supporting the spending restrictions, the Court endorsed the latter approach.

The Dark Side of Egalitarianism: Justice McLachlin's Break with the Court

While the defence of spending restrictions makes sense in theory, in practice it does not necessarily bring about a more robust democracy. In fact, it could have the opposite effect, despite being cloaked in the garb of promoting equality. One's conclusion in this regard depends on the lens through which one views competition in the political marketplace.

Chief Justice McLachlin noted this in her dissent from the *Harper* majority. She echoed comments made by Justices Antonin Scalia and Anthony Kennedy in their dissent from the American Court's decision in *McConnell v. Federal Election Commission*. There, the American Court arrived at the same conclusion and split along the same lines as the Canadian Court did in *Harper*.

McLachlin maintained in *Harper* that if the government were to impose restraints on political speech (qua political spending) it would have to demonstrate that the spending restrictions remedied an identifiable harm to the political process that had resulted from unrestricted spending. In her opinion, the government had not done so:

> The dangers posited are wholly hypothetical. The Attorney General presented no evidence that wealthier Canadians—alone or in concert—will dominate political debate during the electoral period absent limits. It offered only the hypothetical possibility that, without limits on citizen

spending, problems could arise. If, as urged by the Attorney General, wealthy Canadians are poised to hijack this country's election process, an expectation of some evidence to that effect is reasonable. Yet none was presented. This minimizes the Attorney General's assertions of necessity and lends credence to the argument that the legislation is an overreaction to a non-existent problem.[54]

At first, it seems that McLachlin would have joined the *Harper* majority. The opinion echoes those voiced in the opinions she joined in *Figueroa* and *Libman*. The right to vote may be limited if it is done so in a manner that promotes its meaningful exercise.[55] The franchise is meaningful to the extent it is cast in a political environment characterized by diversity of opinions and information. Thus, in the same way the Court struck down laws that hampered the proliferation of political parties in *Figueroa* and diversity of political expression in *Libman*, one would have expected the Court to perhaps strike down the restriction of speech in *Harper*. It did not.

The difference in *Harper* was that all the criteria for justifying an infringement on the franchise seemed to have been addressed. Third-party spending restrictions were justified because they promoted an "equality of volume" of political speech and, as a result, ensured that a few speakers would not drown out others. Thus, the campaign spending limits seemed to promote the meaningful exercise of the franchise that McLachlin had endorsed in her earlier opinions. Yet, she and Justices Ian Binnie and John Major dissented.

In *Harper*, McLachlin saw a more subtle and correspondingly more ominous threat to democracy and the meaningful exercise of the franchise than that posed in earlier cases. To a point, the *Harper* majority appears to stand for the principle that the more powerful political actors should not be allowed to monopolize the political arena:

[S]pending limits seek to protect two groups. First, the limits seek to protect the Canadian electorate by ensuring that it is possible to hear from all groups and thus promote a more informed vote.... [Where] third party advertising seeks to systematically manipulate the voter, the Canadian electorate may be seen as more vulnerable.

[T]he second group protected by the legislation are candidates and political parties.... [A]ll political parties, whether large or small, are "capable of acting as a vehicle for the participation of individual citizens in the public discourse that animates the determination of social policy." Thus, regardless of their size, political parties are important to the democratic process. Nevertheless, neither candidates nor political parties can be said to be vulnerable.[56]

However, McLachlin argued that constraining powerful interest groups actually ends up reducing the political efficacy of all groups in society—including the small weaker ones—because it strengthens the relative power of the government vis-à-vis *all* political groups.

Some observers celebrate such campaign spending legislation because it seems to aid less wealthy or less powerful political actors.[57] However, the spending restrictions in *Harper* compare to the laws challenged in *Libman* and *Figueroa* in a vitally important manner: They insulated incumbent political powers (parties or individuals) from political competition. Under the guise of promoting equality within civil society (by constraining the influence of the more wealthy or powerful), the spending restrictions constrain the capacity of all political actors to challenge entrenched incumbents.

This was not lost on Chief Justice McLachlin. She argued that the spending limits imposed by the 2000 Canada Elections Act were so low that they prevented citizens from "effectively communicating their views on election issues to their fellow citizens, restricting them instead to minor local communication. As such, they represent a serious incursion on free expression in the political realm."[58] This attack on free expression is as damaging to the effective exercise of the franchise as the assault on minor parties struck down by the Court in *Figueroa*. By constraining political voices in the electorate, the spending restrictions diminish the diversity of information and viewpoint that is vital to the effective and meaningful exercise of the franchise. As McLachlin stated:

> The *Canada Elections Act* undercuts the right to listen by withholding from voters an ingredient that is critical to their individual and collective deliberation: substantive analysis and commentary on political issues of the day. The spending limits impede the ability of citizens to communicate with one another through public fora and media during elections and curtail the diversity of perspectives heard and assessed by the electorate. Because citizens cannot mount effective national television, radio and print campaigns, the only sustained messages voters see and hear during the course of an election campaign are from political parties.[59]

Since section 350 prevented citizens (through their third parties and interest groups) from mounting effective challenges to the government, the spending restrictions enhanced the entrenchment of incumbent powers. Voters were now left with two principal sources of political information: the parties and the mass media. McLachlin argued that this arrangement mutes political opposition and speech in the same way as channelling political discussion through one of the two referendum committees in Libman:

> It is no answer to say that the citizen can speak through a registered political party. The citizen may hold views not espoused by a registered party. The citizen has a right to communicate those views. The right to do so is essential to the effective debate upon which our democracy rests, and lies at the core of the free expression guarantee.[60]

Limiting the capacity of large or wealthy private organizations to use their resources to participate in political debate may enhance the political power of smaller political groups relative to their larger competitors in civil society. In this respect, it may actually diversify the opinion and information to which voters are exposed and, thereby, enhance the meaningful exercise of the franchise. However, as McLachlin pointed out in Harper, it also exacerbates the relative inequalities between incumbent political powers and the rest of civil society and thereby mutes the capacity of the electorate as a whole to challenge the government. In this respect, the imposition of equality by the spending restrictions had the same deleterious impact on the exercise of the franchise that it did in Libman because it failed to promote broad political expression. The spending restrictions offer dissenters little if their only avenue of political discourse is through the political parties (or other established political actors) they wish to challenge.

Thus, McLachlin saw two threats to the meaningful exercise of the franchise in all three cases (Libman, Figueroa, and Harper). First, the government attempted to limit diversity of opinion. Second, perhaps more important and more glaringly obvious in Harper, the government, under the cover of promoting equality and restricting individual rights, was actually insulating itself from political competition.

In this respect, McLachlin saw the same threat posed to political liberty that Alexis de Tocqueville described in Democracy in America. In explaining why (and lamenting that) democracies prefer equality to liberty, Tocqueville explained that the desire for equality lends itself to despotism.[61] This is not to say that Parliament has despotic aspirations. Yet, insofar as a government that is less accountable and less subject to popular control is correspondingly less democratic and more despotic, the comparison to Tocqueville's vision is quite apt. Thus, McLachlin abandoned the majority in *Harper* because the other members of the Court did not see that a vote cast in a political environment that was diverse, yet controlled, would be meaningless because the vote would pose less of a threat to the government.

An American Parallel: The Canadianization of American Electoral Law?

The *Harper* decision and McLachlin's dissent embodied a debate almost identical to that in *McConnell v. Federal Election Commission* (2003), where the American Supreme Court used remarkably similar reasoning to uphold various aspects of the Bipartisan Campaign Reform Act (BCRA).[62] The Court supported congressional efforts to remove the appearance of corruption from the political process. While BCRA engendered no shortage of controversy, the key provisions for the purposes of this analysis concerned the restrictions on "soft money" expenditures made by political parties that are not directly related to candidates' campaigns and electioneering communications.[63]

The Court's support for BCRA's restrictions echoed the reasoning of the *Harper* majority. The Court ruled that unfettered speech could actually cause a palpable harm to the political process:

> Because the electoral process is the very "means through which a free society democratically translates political speech into concrete governmental action," contribution limits, like other measures aimed at protecting the integrity of the process, tangibly benefit public participation in political debate. For that reason, when reviewing Congress' decision to enact contribution limits, "there is no place for a strong presumption against constitutionality."[64]

The American Court was as deferential toward Congress as its Canadian counterpart was toward Parliament: "Take away Congress' authority to regulate the appearance of undue influence and 'the cynical assumption that large donors call the tune could jeopardize the willingness of voters to take part in democratic governance.'"[65]

Thus, the American Court not only supported congressional efforts to purge the electoral system of corruption, it also supported Congress's desire to remove the corrupting influences associated with gross disparity of economic power:

Many years ago we observed that "[t]o say that Congress is without power to pass appropriate legislation to safeguard ... an election from the improper use of money to influence the result is to deny to the nation in a vital particular the power of self protection." We abide by that conviction in considering Congress' most recent effort to confine the ill effects of aggregated wealth on our political system.[66]

The American Court had clearly evolved markedly from the narrow approach it took regarding political corruption in *Buckley*. A Court that had once rejected Congress's desire to equalize political influence now stated:

> [P]laintiffs conceive of corruption too narrowly. Our cases have firmly established that Congress' legitimate interest extends beyond preventing simple cash-for-votes corruption to curbing "undue influence on an officeholder's judgment, or the appearance of such influence." Many of the "deeply disturbing examples" of corruption cited by this Court in *Buckley* to justify FECA's contribution limits were not episodes of vote buying, but evidence that various corporate interests had given substantial donations to gain access to high-level government officials.[67]

The American Court's acknowledgment that the appearance of corruption (brought about by inequality of political influence) would diminish the likelihood of voter participation and the vibrancy of the democratic process was not a deviation from its prior opinions. Instead, it represented the continuance of a steady evolution away from the individualism some see in *Buckley*.

This evolution is clearly demonstrated in the American Court's decision in *Nixon v. Shrink Missouri* (2000).[68] There, the Court sustained several campaign spending restrictions that Missouri had imposed on its state legislative elections. In his concurrence, Justice Stephen Breyer offered a thoughtful explanation of the place *Buckley* held in the Court's campaign finance decisions.

Breyer noted that *Buckley* required the Court to balance constitutionally protected interests that "lie on both sides of the legal question."[69] On the one hand, he argued, "a decision to contribute money to a campaign is a matter of First Amendment concern—not because money is speech (it is not); but because it *enables* speech" (emphasis in original).[70] As well, he noted, spending restrictions "protect the integrity of the electoral process—the means through which a free society democratically translates political speech into concrete governmental action."[71] He explained that "by limiting the size of the largest contributions such restrictions aim to democratize the influence that money itself may bring to bear upon the electoral process."[72]

Breyer's approach to campaign spending is therefore cast in terms of what he perceives to be a broader right of voters to participate meaningfully in the political process. Accordingly, in a passage that deserves to be quoted at length, he compares spending restrictions to other aspects of the Constitution that are designed to regulate and balance political debate.

> I recognize that *Buckley* used language that could be interpreted to the contrary. It said, for example, that it rejected "the concept that government may restrict the speech of some elements of our society in order to enhance the relative voice of others." But those words cannot be taken literally. The Constitution often permits restrictions on the speech of some in order to prevent a few from drowning out the many—in Congress, for example, where constitutionally protected debate, Art. I, § 6, is limited to provide every Member an equal opportunity to express his or her views. Or in elections, where the Constitution tolerates numerous restrictions on ballot access, limiting the political rights of some so as to make effective the political rights of the entire electorate. Regardless, as the result in *Buckley* made clear, the statement does not automatically invalidate a statute that seeks a fairer electoral debate through contribution limits, nor should it forbid the Court to take account of the competing constitutional interests just mentioned.

> In such circumstances—where a law significantly implicates competing constitutionally protected interests in complex ways—the Court has closely scrutinized the statute's impact on those interests, but refrained from employing a simple test that effectively presumes unconstitutionality. Rather, it has balanced interests. And in practice that has meant asking whether the statute burdens any one such interest in a manner out of proportion to the statute's salutary effects upon the others (perhaps, but not necessarily, because of the existence of a clearly superior, less restrictive alternative). Where a legislature has significantly greater institutional expertise, as, for example, in the field of election regulation, the Court in practice defers to empirical legislative judgments—at least where that deference does not risk such constitutional evils as, say, permitting incumbents to insulate themselves from effective electoral challenge. This approach is that taken in fact by *Buckley* for contributions, and is found generally where competing constitutional interests are implicated, such as privacy.[73]

Thus, Breyer asserted that the Supreme Court did not regard the individual speech right (in terms of campaign spending) as an absolute. Instead, it is an instrument through which the collective speech of the polity and the calibre of the democratic process can be enhanced. In this respect, the *McConnell* decision is in keeping with the broader spirit of *Buckley* and the balancing that characterized the evolution of the Court's campaign spending law in the three decades after *Buckley* was decided.

While *McConnell* and earlier decisions like *Shrink Missouri* indicate that the American Court is not the bastion of individualism that some scholars have suggested, the decision to sustain campaign spending restrictions in *McConnell* did meet with spirited dissenting opinions from Justices Kennedy and Scalia. These were not cast in strictly libertarian terms. Instead, they anticipated McLachlin's dissent in *Harper*.

The dissenters questioned Congress's desire to restrict speech that had no clear potential to corrupt the political process. As Justice Kennedy noted: "When one recognizes that [the challenged provisions] do not serve the interest the anticorruption rationale contemplates, [they begin] to look very much like an incumbency protection plan. That impression is worsened by the fact that Congress exempted its officeholders from the more stringent prohibitions imposed on party officials."[74]

The dissenters made two points. Justice Kennedy took a very practical approach to BCRA. He did not believe that the concept of corruption could be expanded beyond the realm of quid pro quo exchanges of favours. Therefore, he was unwilling to extend it to include inequality of political influence. Anticipating McLachlin's dissent in *Harper*, Kennedy argued that since there was no clear connection between issue advertising and the notion of quid pro quo corruption, there was no basis on which to restrict these advertisements. Kennedy explains:

In *Buckley*, the Court held that one, and only one, interest justified the significant burden on the right of association involved there: eliminating, or preventing, actual corruption or the appearance of corruption stemming from contributions to candidates.

Placing *Buckley*'s anticorruption rationale in the context of the federal legislative power yields the following rule: Congress' interest in preventing corruption provides a basis for regulating federal candidates' and officeholders' receipt of *quids*, whether or not the candidate or officeholder corruptly received them. Conversely, the rule requires the Court to strike down campaign finance regulations when they do not add regulation to "actual or apparent *quid pro quo* arrangements." [75]

Adhering to the standard set in *Buckley*, Kennedy argued that there is a difference between *undue* influence that comes with quid pro quo corruption and *inequality* of influence that may arise because some speakers, interest groups, or lobbyists are simply more adept or effective than others:

> The very aim of *Buckley*'s standard, however, was to define undue influence by reference to the presence of *quid pro quo* involving the officeholder. The Court, in contrast, concludes that access, without more, proves influence is undue. Access, in the Court's view, has the same legal ramifications as actual or apparent corruption of officeholders. This new definition of corruption sweeps away all protections for speech that lie in its path. [76]

Thus, Kennedy foreshadowed Chief Justice McLachlin: Absent any evidence that unfettered spending resulted in corruption or a diminished democratic process, he was unwilling to support spending restrictions.

Incumbent Entrenchment

A second basis for dissent in *McConnell* addressed a more subtle but equally pernicious threat to democracy. First, the dissenters noted that the spending restrictions forced participants in the political process to channel their speech through preferred routes—routes that were subject to government control. Again anticipating Chief Justice McLachlin, Justice Kennedy noted:

> The *First Amendment* guarantees our citizens the right to judge for themselves the most effective means for the expression of political views and to decide for themselves which entities to trust as reliable speakers. Significant portions of Titles I and II of the Bipartisan Campaign Reform Act of 2002 constrain that freedom. These new laws force speakers to abandon their own preference for speaking through parties and organizations. And they provide safe harbor to the mainstream press, suggesting that the corporate media alone suffice to alleviate the burdens the Act places on the rights and freedoms of ordinary citizens. [77]

Justice Scalia was even more critical. Besides funnelling political speech through preferred channels, BCRA also quelled dissent and criticism of the

114

government. The restrictions on attack ads in the waning weeks of campaigns were clearly designed to protect incumbents from criticism:

> We are governed by Congress, and this legislation prohibits the criticism of Members of Congress by those entities most capable of giving such criticism loud voice: national political parties and corporations, both of the commercial and the not-for-profit sort. It forbids pre-election criticism of incumbents by corporations, even not-for-profit corporations, by use of their general funds; and forbids national-party use of "soft" money to fund "issue ads" that incumbents find so offensive.[78]

Scalia also demonstrated that treating political actors *equally* is not the same as treating them *fairly*:

> To be sure, the legislation is evenhanded: It similarly prohibits criticism of the candidates who oppose Members of Congress in their reelection bids. But as everyone knows, this is an area in which evenhandedness is not fairness. If *all* electioneering were evenhandedly prohibited, incumbents would have an enormous advantage. Likewise, if incumbents and challengers are limited to the same quantity of electioneering, incumbents are favored. In other words, *any* restriction upon a type of campaign speech that is equally available to challengers and incumbents tends to favor incumbents.[79]

Thus, while the BCRA restrictions levelled the political playing field for actors outside the government, they also amplified the relative power of governmental officials vis-à-vis the society at large. In this respect, Justices Scalia and Kennedy arrived at the same conclusion that Justice McLachlin would make six months later in her dissent in *Harper*.

Convergence in American and Canadian Judicial Thought

McLachlin's defection (along with Major and Binnie) from the Canadian Court majority is an especially important event in Canadian jurisprudence. It demonstrates the extent to which her jurisprudential vision of the political process has evolved, or at least the extent to which she and the Court majority have never actually understood one another. Her suspicion of the campaign spending limitations in *Harper* demonstrates a willingness to engage in more exacting scrutiny of governmental motives than her colleagues.

While the Court maintained in the *Saskatchewan Reference* and its other decisions that a certain amount of deference is due to Parliament when it is

115

balancing competing visions of the collective good and individual assertions of rights, McLachlin made clear in *Harper* that such deference had to be conditional. The McLachlin-led Court indicated in *Figueroa* and *Libman* that the Court would not defer to a Parliamentary infringement of individual rights simply because it is grounded in a collective vision of equality. McLachlin reiterated this in *Harper*, but did so in dissent.

The Canadian Court is clearly divided concerning the definition of "effective representation" and a "meaningful" vote. To remedy this division, the Court acknowledges that it must "reconcile the right to meaningfully participate in elections under s. 3 with the right to freedom of expression under s. 2(*b*)" of the Charter.[80] This is hardly a commitment to an egalitarian vision. Instead, it demonstrates that the members of the Court are engaged in an ongoing discussion concerning the best manner to balance competing visions of democratic rights.

Thus, the evolution of McLachlin's thought is driven by a pragmatism and growing skepticism of legislative motive. It may be acceptable to dilute voting power a little (in terms of redistribution in the *Saskatchewan Reference*), but not as much when it comes to blunting political competition (in terms of minor political parties in *Figueroa*), or outright disenfranchisement (*Sauvé*). Different aspects of democratic theory can be used to defend or challenge any of these decisions. In any event, McLachlin has now asserted that the legislature must support limits on political rights such as speech with "a *clear and convincing* demonstration that they are necessary, do not go too far, and enhance more than harm the democratic process" (emphasis added).[81]

This very issue pervaded the American Supreme Court's 2006 campaign spending decision, *Randall v. Sorrell*. In striking down Vermont's contribution and spending restrictions, the Court (led by Justice Breyer) said that "contribution limits might *sometimes* work more harm to protected First Amendment interests than their anticorruption objectives could justify" (emphasis in original).[82]

Breyer acknowledged on the one hand that "in practice, the legislature is better equipped to make [judgments] related to the costs and nature of running for office." However, he said that respect for the legislature's collective expertise was not a carte blanche endorsement of any electoral regulation because

[c]ontribution limits that are too low can also harm the electoral process by preventing challengers from mounting effective campaigns against incumbent offceholders, thereby reducing democratic accountability. Were

we to ignore that fact, a statute that seeks to regulate campaign contributions could itself prove to be an obstacle to the very electoral fairness it seeks to promote.[83]

Most members of the Court addressed the threat of incumbent entrenchment. In fact, Justice Clarence Thomas in his concurrence, and Justice David Souter in his dissent, both acknowledged that incumbent protection at the expense of political competition was an important consideration in their analysis of the spending and contribution restrictions.

Insofar as the American and Canadian campaign spending decisions resonate closely, it is no longer accurate to say that they lie at opposite extremes of a libertarian-egalitarian spectrum. Instead, they have converged to the extent that members of both courts (led by McLachlin in Canada and by Kennedy, Scalia, and Breyer in the United States) are now willing to offer only qualified deference to the legislature when dealing with the regulation of the electoral process. These justices acknowledge that it is no longer clear whether "the legislature" speaks for "the state" or the "collective interest" of the nation, or whether it is simply a temporal governmental majority in "the state's" clothing using an egalitarian cover to disguise attempts to diminish the capacity of the polity to constrain the government.

This does not lend itself to a consistent theory of judicial review. What constitutes a "meaningful vote" depends on the relative weights assigned by a particular judge to the diverse aspects of democratic thought. Distrust of the legislature is grounded in neither a libertarian or egalitarian conception of the franchise or theory of democracy. Instead, it is based on a desire to protect the right to cast a meaningful vote and otherwise participate meaningfully in a fair and open political marketplace. The spending decisions in both countries indicate that whatever we call the two courts' current common mindset, policing the representative process and protecting the integrity of the franchise requires courts to approach these cases in a pragmatic manner—not one bound by the constraints of a particular theoretical vision.

Notes

1   This chapter is drawn from our article, "The Evolution of and Convergence in the Canadian and American Supreme Courts' Electoral Jurisprudence," forthcoming in *McGill Law Journal*.

2   *Buckley v. Valeo*, 424 U.S. 1 (1974).

3   Ibid., 21.

4   To clarify, the Canadian Court refers to such spending as "third-party spending."
     We will try to avoid using this latter term whenever possible to avoid confusing it
     with spending by what Americans tend to refer to as "third parties," which in the
     Canadian context would refer to "minor parties."

5   *Buckley v. Valeo*, 47–48, internal citations omitted.

6   See endnote 11 below.

7   *Buckley v. Valeo*, note 54.

8   Ibid., 48–49, internal citations omitted.

9   The Court did, however, ignore an important problem with the contribution restric-
     tions. Insofar as the campaign finance scheme in FECA gave the Democrats and
     Republicans privileged access to campaign funds in advance of an election, nascent
     third parties had to wait until after the election and would receive reimbursement
     only if they garnered at least 5 per cent of the presidential vote. In this way, the
     campaign finance scheme did indeed limit the potential diversity of political debate
     that the Court seemed to value so highly. Yet, the Court noted:

     Third parties have been completely incapable of matching the major parties' ability
     to raise money and win elections. Congress was, of course, aware of this fact of
     American life, and thus was justified in providing both major parties full funding
     and all other parties only a percentage of the major-party entitlement. Identical
     treatment of all parties, on the other hand, would not only make it easy to raid the
     United States Treasury, it would also artificially foster the proliferation of splinter
     parties. The Constitution does not require the Government to finance the efforts of
     every nascent political group, merely because Congress chose to finance the efforts
     of the major parties (*Buckley*, 98, internal citations omitted).

     As we discuss below, the issue of preferential treatment for incumbents arose in later
     cases and was a key aspect of Justice McLachlin's dissent in *Harper*.

10   Patrick Monahan, *Politics and the Constitution: The Charter, Federalism and the
     Supreme Court of Canada* (Toronto: Carswell, 1987), 134–35.

11   Colin Feasby, "*Libman v. Quebec (A.G.)* and the Administration of the Process of
     Democracy under the Charter: The Emerging Egalitarian Model," *McGill Law Journal*
     44 (1999): 5–39; Colin Feasby, "The Supreme Court of Canada's Political Theory
     and the Constitutionality of the Political Finance Regime," in *Party Funding and
     Campaign Spending in International Perspective*, ed. Samuel Issacharoff and K.D.
     Ewing (Oxford: Hart Publishing, 2006); Heather MacIvor, "The Charter of Rights
     and Party Politics: The Impact of the Supreme Court Ruling in *Figueroa v. Canada
     (Attorney General)*," Montreal: Institute for Research on Public Policy, *Choices* 10
     (2004): 2–26.

12   Frederick Schauer, "Judicial Review of the Devices of Democracy," *Columbia Law
     Review* 94 (1994): 1326–47.

13   Ibid., 1341.

14   Feasby, "The Emerging Egalitarian Model," 20.

15   Ibid., 21.

16   Ibid.

17   Ibid.

18   Ibid., 8.

19 Ibid., 10–11, citing O. Fiss, *The Irony of Free Speech* (Cambridge: Harvard University Press, 1996); C. Sunstein, *Democracy and the Problem of Free Speech* (Toronto: Maxwell Macmillan, 1993); and O. Fiss, "Money and Politics," *Columbia Law Review* 97 (1997): 2470.

20 Ibid., 19.

21 Ibid.

22 *Libman v. Quebec (Attorney General)*, [1997] 3 S.C.R. 569 at para. 40.

23 Feasby, "The Emerging Egalitarian Model," 31.

24 *Libman v. Quebec*, paras. 40–41.

25 Ibid., para. 77.

26 These sections required that parties nominate at least 50 candidates for Parliament to qualify as a "registered" political party and be able to issue tax receipts for contributions.

27 MacIvor, "The Charter of Rights and Party Politics," 11, 13.

28 Ibid., 5.

29 Feasby, "The Political Finance Regime," 251–52.

30 In fact, MacIvor states that "*Libman* demonstrated that the libertarian approach was a nonstarter at the Supreme Court of Canada." MacIvor, "The Charter of Rights and Party Politics," 13.

31 Feasby, "The Political Finance Regime," 252.

32 *Figueroa v. Canada*, [2003] 1 S.C.R. 912 at para. 28.

33 Ibid., para. 30.

34 Ibid., para. 54.

35 See also Christopher D. Bredt and Markus F. Kremer, "Section 3 of the Charter: Democratic Rights at the Supreme Court of Canada," *National Journal of Constitutional Law* 17 (2006): 20–70.

36 *Figueroa v. Canada*, para. 26.

37 MacIvor, "The Charter of Rights and Party Politics," 7.

38 *Figueroa v. Canada*, para. 101.

39 Ibid., paras. 108–09.

40 Ibid., para. 33.

41 See generally, Feasby, "The Political Finance Regime."

42 *Figueroa v. Canada*, para. 114.

43 Ibid., para. 117.

44 Bredt and Kremer ("Democratic Rights at the Supreme Court") make a similar point, questioning why the Court allows dilution of voting power in some cases (urban voters in the *Saskatchewan Reference*) but not in others (minor party supporters in *Figueroa*).

45 *Figueroa v. Canada*, para. 101.

46 Ibid., para. 181.

47 *Harper v. Canada*, [2004] 1 S.C.R. 827.

48 Ibid., para. 62.

49 Ibid., para. 63.

50 Ibid., para. 91.

51 Ibid., para. 72, internal citations omitted.

52 Ibid., para. 109–10.

53 Ibid., para. 62.

54 Ibid., para. 34.

55 See *Figueroa v. Canada*, paras. 33–37.

56 *Harper v. Canada*, paras. 80–81, internal citations omitted.

57 See, e.g., "Victory for Democracy," *Toronto Star*, 20 May 2004; "The Court Shushes the Rich," *The Globe and Mail*, 19 May 2004.

58 *Harper v. Canada*, para. 10.

59 Ibid., para. 19.

60 Ibid., para. 21.

61 See Alexis de Tocqueville, *Democracy in America*, ed. P. Bradley (New York: Vintage Books, 1945), 2:109.

62 *McConnell v. Federal Election Commission*, 540 U.S. 93 (2003).

63 See generally, Robert Bauer, *More Soft Money, Hard Law* (Washington, DC: Perkins Coie LLP, 2003).

64 *McConnell v. Federal Election Commission*, 137.

65 Ibid., 144.

66 Ibid., 223–24.

67 Ibid., 150.

68 *Nixon v. Shrink Missouri Government PAC*, 528 U.S. 377 (2000).

69 Ibid., 400.

70 Ibid.

71 Ibid., 401.

72 Ibid.

73 Ibid., 402–03, internal citations omitted.

74 *McConnell v. Federal Election Commission*, 306.

75 Ibid., 294.

76 Ibid.

77 Ibid., 287.

78 Ibid., 248.

79 Ibid., 249.

80 *Harper v. Canada*, para. 50.

81 *Harper v. Canada*, para. 21.

82 *Randall v. Sorrell*, 126 S. Ct. 2479, 2491–92 (2006).

83 Ibid., 14.

chapter five

Judicial Struggles with Democracy and the Unbearable Lightness of Process

As this book went to press, two cases in both nations demonstrated that the skepticism of legislative motive was indeed growing in both supreme courts. In *R. v. Bryan* (2007), the Canadian Court split 5–4 and dismissed a challenge to section 329 of the Canada Elections Act, which prohibits the transmission of electoral results in one riding to another before the closing of polls in the latter.[1] During the 2000 parliamentary election, Paul Charles Bryan had posted election results from Atlantic Canada on a website. He thereby made them available across Canada despite the fact that polling stations were still open in the Western provinces. He was fined $1,000 for violating section 329.

The majority, led by Justice Michel Bastarache, deferred to the government's desire to ensure that all voters go to the polls with the same type, quality, and amount of information. Accordingly, the infringement on free speech imposed by the broadcast restriction was acceptable in light of the government's desire to protect the integrity of the electoral process and to maintain public confidence in the fairness of the rules by which elections are conducted. The dissenting justices, led by Justice Rosalie Abella (and joined by the chief justice), asserted that the government had not provided enough evidence to justify section 329's infringement on free speech.

The dissent acknowledged that ensuring "that electors in different parts of the country have access to the same information before they go to the polls" is a "pressing and substantial" governmental objective.[2] However, they argued the publication ban was not necessary to achieve this goal. Further, it entailed much more than a "minimal" impairment of the right to speak. The right at issue, said Abella, is "the right of the media and others to publish election results in a timely fashion and the right of all Canadians to receive it."[3] Insofar as communicating and receiving election results is a core democratic right that is an "essential" part of the democratic process, "clear and convincing evidence is required" to justify limiting the broadcast or availability of political information.[4] The harm to the Charter, Abella argued, was "demonstrable." Yet, the "benefits of the ban are not."[5] Section 329 therefore failed not only the rational basis test but also any test of proportionality under *Oakes*.

More recently, in *Federal Election Commission v. Wisconsin Right to Life* (WRTL) (2007) the US Court sustained a challenge to the same section 203 of the Bipartisan Campaign Reform Act (BCRA) that had been challenged and sustained in *McConnell v. FEC* (2003). The decision itself was quite narrow. By a margin of 5–4, the Court ruled that the ban on express advocacy contained in section 203 did not apply to the advertisements that WRTL had wished to run during the 30-day blackout period before the 2004 federal primary elections in Wisconsin.

Even though he agreed with the majority ruling, Justice Antonin Scalia wrote a separate concurrence in which he urged that section 203 should be overturned. Again, he (like Justices Abella, Beverley McLachlin, and the other Canadian dissenters in *Bryan*) asserted that there was no evidence that the electoral process was threatened by the political speech and spending that section 203 sought to control. To the contrary, he argued, the evidence suggested that, once again, incumbents had passed the law to protect themselves.

> There is wondrous irony to be found in both the genesis and the consequences of BCRA. In the fact that the institutions it was designed to muzzle—unions and nearly all manner of corporations—for all the "corrosive and distorting effects" of their "immense aggregations of wealth," were utterly impotent to prevent the passage of this legislation that forbids them to criticize candidates (including incumbents).[6]

Thus, the skeptical dissenters in *McConnell* now comprised the majority in WRTL (thanks in part to the arrival of two new court members, Chief Justice

John Roberts and Associate Justice Samuel Alito). Similarly, whereas Chief Justice McLachlin was joined by only two other dissenters in *Harper*, she was joined by three in *Bryan*. Thus, as the two supreme courts continue to engage in the same debates about the democratic process, the skepticism of legislative motives is increasing as well.

Insofar as this growing skepticism is fuelled by a desire to keep the political marketplace open and preserve the meaning of the franchise, the courts of both nations will most certainly remain the objects of criticism. On the one hand, it makes it more difficult for judges to give the legislature the option of having the last word in Peter Hogg and Allison Bushell's dialogue. On the other, since neither court has yet to provide a clear definition of what constitutes a meaningful vote, they engender criticism for having no well-defined basis for striking down electoral regulations.

We believe that the absence thus far of a clear theoretical basis for challenging the legislature's motives indicates nothing more than that the two courts are developing their jurisprudence incrementally. This is a clear manifestation of the dialogic approach to constitutional interpretation. The uncertainty that may arise from the absence of a coherent judicial vision of democracy can be managed, so long as the justices approach election law questions modestly. For the most part, the skeptics on both courts have done so by voicing their concerns about the challenged electoral laws with calls for the legislature to provide more convincing evidence on which to justify the restrictions on spending and speech.

Nonetheless, in one important respect, the Canadian Supreme Court has extended its skepticism one step further, and therefore has remained radically distinct from its American counterpart when addressing questions of election law. Strikingly, in several cases—including *Sauvé 2*—the Canadian Court has demonstrated a willingness to police not only the democratic *process*, but also its *outputs*. This activism threatens not only to undermine the basis for any dialogue in the sense meant by advocates of this theory in Canada but to fundamentally alter the nature of Canadian democracy itself.

A Meaningful Vote

The debates and discussions in the decisions of both courts indicate that the justices generally agree that voting must be meaningful, but disagree about the specific definition of a meaningful vote and how best to protect it. In broad strokes, a meaningful vote has the following components.

1. One vote counts as much as any other. As we saw in the *Saskatchewan Reference* and the US Court's case law, individual votes should have more or less the same impact on the electoral process. As well, political groups should have a fair chance to gain representation.
2. Meaningful votes should be informed. That is, voters should have access to and be able to acquire information about electoral issues and choices to inform their election-day decisions. As both courts indicated in the campaign spending decisions, and the Canadian Court said in *Libman*, information should not be channelled through particular groups or filters. The marketplace of ideas should be free. In this same spirit, the volume of some ideas may need to be controlled to ensure that other ideas are not drowned out.
3. Meaningful votes should count collectively as well as individually. That is, they should not be cast in an electoral environment whose outcome is preconditioned in any way. From the beginning of American electoral case law, this has meant that electoral districts should not be gerrymandered to prevent certain groups from gaining representation. As demonstrated more recently in both nations' campaign spending decisions, this means that voters and nonincumbent candidates should be able to challenge incumbent political actors. The government should not be able to insulate itself from competition in the political marketplace. Instead, the political marketplace should be competitive.
4. Finally, a meaningful vote is one that is cast in a legislative process that is free to evolve through deliberation—within the legislature and via a dialogue with the judiciary. If the courts do not behave modestly (as Justice Stephen Breyer would say), or if they seek to impose what Patrick Monahan described as "the correct answer" on legislative deliberations, they undermine the capacity of the polity to govern itself. In so doing, the vote is rendered less meaningful.

These principles are certainly in keeping with democratic theory and resonate with the concerns of John Hart Ely and Monahan that we discussed in Chapter 1. However, critics have argued that calls for courts to police the political marketplace lack theoretical consistency and clear notions of what, for example, constitutes an ideal level of political competition. While these criticisms may be accurate, they do not render this venture impossible or undesirable.

Do the Courts Need a Theory to Protect the Democratic Process?

Critics argue that the marketplace metaphor is an awkward and imperfect tool for protecting political rights because the parallels that we can draw between voters and consumers, political parties and firms, etc., are not as neat or clean as we would like.[7] Criticisms boil down to the following:

1. Theories of judicial review grounded in notions of "fair political process" are essentially stillborn because their proponents *must* base their vision of a fair political process on some substantive vision of political rights.[8] In this respect, judges cannot help but do what Monahan decried and impose a "right answer" on the legislative process.

2. The comparison made between the economic and political marketplace is at best incomplete, and at worst, simply inapt. As Richard Hasen notes, we lack a "proper yardstick for measuring success (or efficiency) in a political market."[9] As well, we lack a clear notion of how "competitive is competitive enough."[10]

3. Even if we could get around the problem of defining an appropriate level of political competition,[11] different theories of democracy emphasize values that are simply not compatible or easily balanced. Thus, Daniel Lowenstein points out that a judge's preference for individual rights, party-government, or progressive visions of democracy will inevitably lead him or her to resolve a dispute differently than a judge who prefers another aspect of democratic theory.[12]

Despite the market model's shortcomings, critics acknowledge that its focus on policing the political process is "crucial" insofar as it can indicate whether a purported state interest (in regulating the electoral process) is in fact motivated by "self-preservation rather than a desire to promote political stability, antifactionalism, or some other interest."[13] While it may be as difficult to define ideal political competition as it is to identify an ideal level of economic competition, the election law cases in both courts show that it is not so difficult to identify examples of cartel-like behaviour or barriers to competition that do have detrimental impacts on political or economic choice and competition. Collusion among large firms to fix prices, or collusion among major parties to increase the cost of independent candidacies or the cost of creating a new political party diminishes competition. Similarly, channelling speech through only a "oui" or "non" conduit in *Libman*, or limiting criticism of incumbents in *McConnell* or *Harper* clearly entails cartel-like behaviour. Thus, it is not difficult to identify monopoly- or cartel-like behaviour when one sees it.

Insofar as neither nation's constitution offers a clear definition of democratic rights or an endorsement of a particular strain of democratic theory, it is wise for the courts and individual judges to proceed modestly and avoid incorporating a particular vision of democracy into its constitutional interpretation. Had either court chosen to adhere rigidly to a particular vision of democracy (libertarian, egalitarian, etc.,) in its election law decisions, it would have been as guilty of undermining the deliberative capacity of the democratic process as the American Court was in 1905. Then, in *Lochner v. New York*, it struck down a law protecting the health of bakers by restricting the number of hours they could work because, as Justice Oliver Wendell Holmes argued, it did not resonate with "Mr. Herbert Spencer's Social Statics."[14]

Our analysis indicates that the courts did not adhere to a particular egalitarian or libertarian vision of the political process. Particular members of the two courts may have done so in particular cases,[15] but, *in toto*, the courts are increasingly inclined to promote openness and competitiveness without adhering to discrete normative democratic visions. Instead, the courts of both nations have refined their understanding of democratic competition over time.

An Important Difference

Ironically, the greatest difference between the two supreme courts arose in the criminal disenfranchisement cases, where the Canadian Court was the most theoretically rigid and correspondingly least deferential toward the legislature's reasoning. In *Richardson*, the US Court acknowledged that state legislatures might (and were free) to adopt a different vision of democracy and choose *not* to disenfranchise criminals. The US Court was not going to overturn their decisions simply because it preferred a different democratic vision. In *Sauvé 2*, in the absence of a constitutional endorsement of or ban on criminal disenfranchisement, there was actually more room for debate and dialogue about the meaning of the franchise under section 3 of the Charter. However, the Canadian Court chose one version of democratic theory and overruled competing visions that offered reasonable (but not necessarily popular) bases for criminal disenfranchisement.

The American Court's election law jurisprudence has evolved over the better part of half a century of interaction and dialogue with the state legislatures and Congress. The result has been a gradual loosening of the one-person-one-vote rule and a greater accommodation of state legislative attempts (and congressional demands under the Voting Rights Act) to accommodate minority voting rights. Meanwhile, in Canada, while Colin Feasby and Heather MacIvor's original analyes suggested that the Canadian Court used an egalitarian model of democracy to strike down the laws challenged in *Libman* and *Figueroa*, the decisions in *Harper* and *Bryan* demonstrate that the chief justice and the court members who agreed with her did not endorse the egalitarian vision. Similarly, while the US Court has sustained many campaign regulations, it has insisted that Congress and the states demonstrate that the restrictions on spending and speech be aimed at a clear threat to the integrity of the political process. Thus, many members of both courts have been deferential toward the elected branches, and it is clear that the case law is the product of an ongoing conversation about (not a coherent theoretical vision of) the nature of the political process. However, as we demonstrated in the last chapter, a result of this ongoing dialogue has been a growing fear in both supreme courts that the legislatures may engage in cartel-like behaviour and seek to insulate themselves from political competition.

The Canadian Judicial Threat to Democracy and the Dialogue

The fear of incumbents "locking up" the political process clearly undermines judicial justification for behaving modestly and, as Hogg and Bushell cast it, allowing the legislature the option to have the last word—at least when it comes to electoral law. Nonetheless, as we saw in the recent campaign spending decisions in both courts, a judicial demand for more evidence still leaves the legislature the option to respond and craft new legislation. However, in *Sauvé 2* the Canadian Court left the legislature no such option. Instead, the Court presumed to have a clearer vision of democracy than the legislature, going so far as to dismiss countries that disenfranchised criminals as "self-proclaimed" democracies. This aspect of the Canadian Court's jurisprudence has no parallel in the United States Supreme Court decisions. We argue that this approach to the democratic process threatens the dialogic method of constitutional interpretation and the integrity of the democratic process it promotes. It is manifest in several other decisions by the Canadian Court.

Vriend v. Alberta: Correcting an "Improper" Democratic Process

In *Vriend v. Alberta* (1998), the Canadian Supreme Court sustained a challenge to Alberta's Individual Rights Protection Act (IRPA).[16] In the facts of the case, laboratory coordinator Delwin Vriend had admitted his homosexuality at work and was subsequently terminated by his employer, King's University College in Edmonton, because its Christian founding principles did not condone his sexual orientation. Since IRPA did not include sexual orientation as a protected ground for discrimination suits, the Alberta Human Rights Commission dismissed Vriend's appeal. He subsequently challenged the constitutionality of the act's omission of sexual orientation as a protected class.[17]

The Supreme Court declared that IRPA was unconstitutional because it did not include sexual orientation as a protected class. It stated that minorities are entitled not only to be represented and participate in the political process but also to have their demands met (regardless of majority opposition). Speaking for the Court, Justice Frank Iacobucci said this was a clear example of what Monahan described as a "tainted" political process:

[T]he process by which the Alberta Legislature decided to exclude sexual orientation from the IRPA was *inconsistent with democratic principles.* Both the trial judge and all judges in the Court of Appeal agreed that the exclusion of sexual orientation from the IRPA was a conscious and deliberate legislative choice....

[T]he concept of democracy means more than majority rule.... [A] democracy requires that legislators take into account the interests of majorities and minorities alike, all of whom will be affected by the decisions they make. Where the interests of a minority have been denied consideration, especially where that group has historically been the target of prejudice and discrimination, I believe that *judicial intervention is warranted to correct a democratic process that has acted improperly* (emphasis added).[18]

In *Vriend*, the Court manifested impatience with the deliberative incremental process of bargaining among interest groups that characterizes democratic legislation. It took the extraordinary step of declaring that it would "read sexual orientation in" to the text of the act. That is, instead of simply striking the legislation down and leaving it for Alberta to decide whether or not to craft a new version of IRPA that would comport with the Court's ruling, the Court essentially rewrote IRPA.

The Court rejected assertions that IRPA was simply the natural result of bargaining and compromise among competing interest groups mediated by the legislature.[19] Instead, it truncated the deliberative process and imposed what it considered to be "the right answer" on the political process. Yet, Justice Iacobucci said that "reading in" did not truncate the deliberative process. Instead, it engaged the judiciary in a dialogue with the legislature.

Accordingly, if the legislature disagreed with the Supreme Court's ruling, it was entitled and empowered to respond.

> When a court remedies an unconstitutional statute by reading in provisions, no doubt this constrains the legislative process and therefore should not be done needlessly, but only after considered examination. However, in my view, the "parliamentary safeguards" remain. Governments are free to modify the amended legislation by passing exceptions and defences which they feel can be justified under s. 1 of the *Charter*. Thus, when a court reads in, this is not the end of the legislative process because the legislature can pass new legislation in response.... Moreover, the legislators can always turn to s. 33 of the *Charter*, the override provision, which in my view is the ultimate "parliamentary safeguard."[20]

The impatience that characterized *Vriend* was evident again in *Attorney General for Ontario v. M. & H.* (1999).[21] Here the Court declared that section 29 of Ontario's Family Law Act (FLA) violated section 15 of the Charter because it defined "spouse" only in terms of "persons of the opposite sex." The Court decided to read "same-sex couples" into the legislation instead of simply sending it back to the provincial legislature. Since FLA allowed cohabiting heterosexuals to sue for spousal support, the Court ruled that the legislature's failure to extend the right to make such claims to homosexual couples could not withstand constitutional scrutiny.

Ontario had argued that the law was aimed specifically at protecting women who suffered disproportionate economic hardship after divorce and separation.[22] It was not intended to discriminate against homosexuals. Instead, it addressed a particular social problem concerning the welfare of women.

Speaking again for the Court, Justice Iacobucci argued that the legislature's failure to include homosexual couples in the act manifested a discriminatory intent.[23]

> [Ontario] contends that the decision to provide equal status to both sexes under the FLRA, followed by the extension of the right to claim support to opposite-sex common-law couples and the further broadening of the definition of "spouse" under the FLA by reducing the requisite period of cohabitation from five to three years, is significant evidence of incremental progress toward the ideal of equality. Therefore, it is submitted that this Court ought to be wary of interfering with the existing legislation. I disagree. None of the reforms cited by [Ontario] has addressed the equal

rights and obligations of individuals in same-sex relationships. In fact, there is no evidence of any progress with respect to this group since the inception of the spousal support regime. If the legislature refuses to act so as to evolve towards Charter compliance then deference as to the timing of reforms loses its raison d'être.[24]

In the Court's view, deliberative and incremental legislative behaviour was just another way of not legislating. Thus, it rejected the province's evidence that over time it had expanded the scope of the act on the grounds that this expansion had done nothing to address homosexuals.

Justice Iacobucci's concerns about an improperly functioning democratic process were echoed by Justice Peter Cory, who said that the "social cost of leaving this matter undecided would be significant."[25] The problem with this assertion, however, is that the matter *had not* been left undecided. The Ontario government, under the leadership of an NDP premier, had attempted to amend the statutory definition of "spouse." There was a vigorous public and legislative debate on the question, in which gay and lesbian rights activists enjoyed the support of the premier and his cabinet. Nevertheless, the Ontario legislature defeated the amendment in a free vote. The Court altered the law simply because it was not satisfied with the speed of the legislative process.

The Canadian Court's willingness to reverse legislative decisions on the grounds that they are "improper" or carry a high social cost is not limited to claims by minority groups. Consider, for example, the Court's 4–3 decision in *Chaoulli v. Quebec* (2005), invalidating the province's prohibitions against private insurance coverage for services provided through the public health care system.[26]

According to Justice Marie Deschamps, the existence of lengthy waiting lists for certain surgical procedures unjustifiably affected the rights to life and personal inviolability protected under section 1 of the quasi-constitutional Quebec Charter of Rights and Freedoms. Justice Deschamps rejected both the alleged micro- and macrolevel consequences of eliminating the public monopoly on the provision of health care. She indicated that "no study produced or discussed" at trial supported the conclusion that the availability of private insurance would have perverse consequences on individual behaviour in the system;[27] nor did she find adequate evidence that private insurance would lead to increased costs or a general deterioration of the public system.[28] To the contrary, she cited the experience of other OECD countries as evidence that "a number of measures are available ... to protect the integrity of Quebec's health care plan" even with private insurance.[29]

Chief Justice McLachlin, with Justice John Major and Justice Bastarache, concurred with Justice Deschamps's Quebec Charter analysis, but went further in declaring that the prohibition was also invalid under section 7 of the Canadian Charter. According to the chief justice, "access to a waiting list is not access to health care," so that "prohibiting health insurance that would permit ordinary Canadians to access health care, in circumstances where the government is failing to deliver health care in a reasonable manner, thereby increasing the risk of complications and death, interferes with life and security of the person as protected by s. 7 of the *Charter*."[30] Moreover, she found the prohibition "arbitrary," and therefore contrary to the principles of fundamental justice.[31]

The *Chaoulli* case in effect constituted a judicial referendum on the status of two different reports on the state of public health care in Canada: the Romanow and Kirby reports. One report—Romanow—had advocated maintaining a public health care monopoly; the other—Kirby—had advocated increased reliance on private provision. The distribution of judicial references to these reports in the judgments in *Chaoulli* demonstrates their relative impact. References to the Kirby Report outnumbered references to the Romanow Report by 13 to 3 in the 2 majority judgments. By contrast, 12 paragraphs of the dissenting judgment contain references to the Romanow Report. Indeed, to paraphrase Ely, one can easily characterize the outcome in *Chaoulli* as: "We like Kirby, you like Romanow. We win, 4–3. Statutory provision invalidated."[32]

Even more revealing, however, was Justice Deschamps's justification for judicial intervention in the case. "Courts," she argued, "have all the necessary tools ... to find a solution to the problem of waiting lists" and respond to "the urgency of taking concrete action" in the face of a "situation that continues to deteriorate." Governments "cannot choose to do nothing," and when they do, "courts are the last line of defence for citizens."[33] The notion that courts are the last line of defence for citizens generally, rather than for minorities (as one might argue was the case in *Vriend* and *M. & H.*), goes well beyond traditional justifications for aggressive rights-based judicial review. The policy negated in *Chaoulli* reflected a choice made by the very citizens Justice Deschamps sought to protect, and presumably they are best positioned to reverse that choice if they determine that it no longer serves their interests.

Back to the Beginning—Protecting the Unique Canadian Vision of Democracy?

The Court's language in these three cases—*Vriend, M. & H.,* and *Chaoulli*—compares to its approach to prisoner disenfranchisement in *Sauvé* and contrasts starkly with the approach to judicial review that it brought to bear in the other cases dealing with the electoral process. Instead of protecting the integrity of the political process from legislative encroachment, the Court questioned the legitimacy of the process that produced the laws with which it did not agree.[34]

In particular, "reading in" imposes a law on the people that their representatives may never have generated. It discourages legislators from bargaining effectively because they know that a legislative compromise (or any legislation that the judiciary would regard as less than complete or perfect) is subject to "correction" by the judiciary. This creates a disincentive to work incrementally. In short, the threat of the judiciary "reading in" reduces the incentive for legislative bargaining because the process and outcome can be wrested away by the judiciary.[35] If they fail to achieve what the Court regards as ideal legislation, the Court may read in substance that might have prevented even the imperfect law from ever passing.

"Political debate," says Monahan, "is not valued because it will necessarily yield right answers to issues of political morality, but because it is a necessary feature of a community defining and revising its own identity."[36] He explained that

> [t]he rights and freedoms of Canadians can be protected most effectively by the political process, rather than the judicial process. It is intellectually fashionable ... to dismiss the political process as unprincipled and arbitrary. Critics of the political process typically rely on a very limited number of historical examples to support their case. Pointing to instances in which majorities have denied the rights of minorities, these critics suggest that the only answer is to hand politics over to the judiciary.[37]

Monahan's view of democratic politics trusts the legislature to generate "good" (if not "right") results over time—but not necessarily immediately.

If the legislature cannot reach consensus, the government might prefer (or be forced) to do nothing or move incrementally toward a legislative goal. Under these circumstances, "no law" (or, we can infer, a law that moves in the right legislative direction) might be the best temporary resolution to a political conflict, even though members of a court might find such a resolution to be unsatisfactory. "Unsatisfactory" does not imply "unconstitutional." Nor does an unsatisfactory legislative resolution or compromise today indicate that no other compromise is possible in the future.

Conclusion: The Crisis of Democracy in the Canadian Court?

The point at which the Canadian and United States courts converged represents a judicial recognition that democratic deliberation requires a delicate balancing of complementary but sometimes competing visions of rights. The dialogic approach to that balance ensures that the definitions of those rights, as well as the legislative process, can be fine-tuned by the judiciary and the legislature.

Accordingly, we note in conclusion that, in some ways, the American Court's approach to the political process appears to be more "Canadian" and dialogic than that taken by the Canadian Court. Despite assertions by Canadian scholars about American individualism, the US Supreme Court has balanced competing conceptions of rights, engaged in a dialogue with the Congress and state legislatures concerning the definition of voting rights, and respected the incremental process of legislative deliberation. The evolution of the Canadian Court's voting rights jurisprudence follows a path similar to that taken by its counterpart to the south. However, the Canadian Court's impatience with the deliberative legislative process presents in some cases an ominous threat to the democratic dialogue envisioned by the Charter.

Notes

1 *R. v. Bryan*, 2007 S.C.C. 12 (March 15).

2 Ibid., para. 104, citing *Harper v. Canada*, para. 132.

3 Ibid., para. 110.

4 Ibid.

5 Ibid., para. 131.

6 *Federal Election Commission v. Wisconsin Right to Life*, 127 S. Ct. 2652 (2007), available at <http://caselaw.lp.findlaw.com/cgi-bin/getcase.pl?court=US&navby=case&vol=000&invol=06-969>.

7 See Michael P. McDonald and John Samples, eds., *The Marketplace of Democracy: Electoral Competition and American Politics* (Washington, DC: Brookings Institution Press, 2006). See also Samuel Issacharoff and Richard Pildes, "Politics as Markets: Partisan Lockups of the Democratic Process," *Stanford Law Review* 50 (1998): 643–717; Samuel Issacharoff, "Gerrymandering and Political Cartels," *Harvard Law Review* 116 (2002): 593–648; Michael Klarman, "The Puzzling Resistance to Political Process Theory," *Virginia Law Review* 77 (1991): 747–832; Robert F. Bauer, "When the Pols Make the Calls: *McConnell*'s Theory of Judicial Deference in the Twilight of *Buckley*," *University of Pennsylvania Law Review* 153 (2004):

5–30; Robert F. Bauer, "Judicial Deference to the Legislature in Campaign Finance Regulation: Justice Breyer's Concept of Active Liberty," available at <http://moresoft moneyhardlaw.com/rev20041129.cfm>; Richard L. Hasen, "The Political Market Metaphor and Election Law: A Comment on Issacharoff and Pildes," *Stanford Law Review* 50 (February 1998): 719–30; Daniel H. Lowenstein, "The Supreme Court Has No Theory of Politics—and Be Thankful for Small Favors," in *The U.S. Supreme Court and the Electoral Process*, ed. David K. Ryden (Washington, DC: Georgetown University Press, 2000). See also Nathaniel Persily, "In Defense of Foxes Guarding Henhouses: The Case for Judicial Acquiescence to Incumbent-Protecting Gerrymanders," 116 *Harvard Law Review* (2002): 649–84. Regarding John Hart Ely's work, see, for example, Laurence H. Tribe, "The Puzzling Persistence of Process-Based Constitutional Theories," *Yale Law Journal* 89 (1979–80): 1064.

8   See Tribe, "Process-Based Constitutional Theories," 1064.

9   Hasen, "The Political Market Metaphor," 720. Richard Hasen notes that judicial inquiry into attempts to "lock up" the political process will be useful only when we know how "competitive is competitive enough." For example, he challenges Issacharoff and Pildes's concerns about partisan duopolies by noting the inconsistency in the political science literature that, on the one hand, celebrated the creation of robust two-party competition in the once one-party South while simultaneously lamenting the lack of competitiveness in the two-party Northern states. In response to Issacharoff and Pildes's criticism of the Supreme Court's support of Minnesota's restriction on fusion candidacies, Hasen asked: "How is it that two-party competition in Minnesota's electoral system is not 'appropriately competitive,' whereas the South's emerging two-party system is 'robust'?" This still begs the question: By what objective standard can a judge or scholar justify striking down any allegedly unfair manipulation or regulation of the political process?

10   Ibid., 730.

11   Ibid., 725.

12   Lowenstein, "No Theory of Politics."

13   Ibid., 728.

14   *Lochner v. New York*, 195 U.S. 45 at 75 (1905).

15   See the Court's assertion of an egalitarian model of politics in *Libman*. See also Justice Louis LeBel's criticism of Chief Justice Beverley McLachlin's individualistic interpretation of rights in *Figueroa*. The chief justice's judgment in *Sauvé 2* is another instance.

16   *Vriend v. Alberta*, [1998] 1 S.C.R. 493.

17   Criticisms of *Vriend* focus in part on the Supreme Court's solicitousness toward groups who, having lost political battles, seek legal means to advance their agendas. Critics point out that the Court's solicitousness toward group rights claims under the Charter is fundamentally at odds with the intentions of the Charter's framers. See F.L. Morton, "Canada's Judge Bork: Has the Counter-Revolution Begun?" *Constitutional Forum* 7 (1996): 121–25; Rainer Knopff and F.L. Morton, *Charter Politics* (Scarborough: Nelson Canada, 1992); Rainer Knopff and F.L. Morton, "Canada's Court Party," in *Rethinking the Constitution*, ed. Anthony Peacock (Ontario: Oxford University Press, 1996); Anthony A. Peacock, "Strange Brew: Tocqueville, Rights and the Technology of Equality," in *Rethinking the Constitution*, ed. Anthony Peacock (Ontario: Oxford University Press, 1996). In Canada, the

Supreme Court has followed a path similar to that of the American Court concerning the expansion of equality rights to unenumerated political groups, but it has cast the terms of its debate differently. Starting with the *BC Motor Vehicle Reference* (1986) and proceeding through *Egan and Nesbit v. The Queen* (1995) and, finally, *Vriend*, the Canadian Court also added substance to the notion of due process in the Charter of Rights and Freedoms, declaring that it would not be bound by a narrow procedurally focused interpretation of section 7.

The Charter specifically promotes multiculturalism and enumerates particular types of groups entitled to protection. Section 27 reads: "This Charter shall be interpreted in a manner consistent with the preservation and enhancement of the multicultural heritage of Canadians." As a result, the Canadian Court has been spared the controversial task of having to develop a list of such groups on its own (as Justice Harlan Fiske Stone of the American Court did in the 1938 *Carolene Products* decision). Thus, in contrast to the American Court's developing a sliding scale of scrutiny to assess the rationale underlying legislation, the Canadian Court has been able to work from a pre-existing list of which groups count for special constitutional protection. However, in *Andrews v. Law Society of British Columbia*, [1989] 1 S.C.R. 143, the Supreme Court took the controversial step of expanding the list of groups that it would recognize (C. Lynn Smith, "Adding a Third Dimension: The Canadian Approach to Constitutional Equality Guarantees," *Law and Contemporary Problems* 55 (1992): 211–34). In addition to recognizing discrimination that might be based on sex, disability, age, national origin, or ethnicity (the criteria set forth in section 15 of the Charter), the Supreme Court concluded that groups or individuals who suffered analogous discrimination would also have standing to challenge litigation (see *Andrews v. Law Society of BC*, 171–175).

18   *Vriend v. Alberta*, paras. 175–78, citing, *inter alia*, Ely and Patrick Monahan.

19   Ibid., paras. 122–23.

20   Ibid., para. 178.

21   *Attorney General for Ontario v. M. & H. (M. & H.)*, [1999] 2 S.C.R. 3.

22   Ibid., paras. 193–213.

23   Ibid., para. 103.

24   Ibid., para. 129.

25   Ibid., paras. 43–45.

26   *Chaoulli v. Quebec*, [2005] 1 S.C.R. 791.

27   Ibid., para. 62.

28   Ibid., para. 66.

29   Ibid., para. 84.

30   Ibid., paras. 123–24.

31   Ibid., para. 153.

32   John Hart Ely, *Democracy and Distrust* (Cambridge: Harvard University Press, 1980), 58.

33   *Chaoulli v. Quebec*, paras. 96–97.

34   Of course, the Canadian Court was divided in these cases as it was in the other cases dealing with the political process. In *M. & H.*, Justice Charles Gonthier accepted Ontario's explanation that the decision to extend benefits to certain aggrieved groups

created no additional responsibility to extend it to other groups. "Legislatures operate incrementally and therefore, cannot be deemed unjust for failing to pass laws
that benefit all possible groups" (*M. & H.*, paras. 230–41).

35   See Mark Tushnet, "Policy Distortion and Democratic Debilitation: Comparative
Illumination of the Countermajoritarian Difficulty," 94 *Michigan Law Review*
(1995): 245–301.

36   Patrick Monahan, *Politics and the Constitution: The Charter, Federalism and the
Supreme Court of Canada* (Toronto: Carswell, 1987), 105.

37   Monahan, *Politics and the Constitution*, 119. The ellipsis reads, "particularly in the
United States." We removed it here because we believe it is no longer accurate and
therefore distracts the reader from Monahan's broader point about the legislature's
superiority at protecting rights.

Bibliography

Aleinikoff, T. Alexander, and Samuel Issacharoff. "Race and Redistricting: Drawing Lines after *Shaw v. Reno.*" *Michigan Law Review* 92 (1993): 588–603.

Bauer, Robert F. "Judicial Deference to the Legislature in Campaign Finance Regulation: Justice Breyer's Concept of Active Liberty." Available at http://moresoftmoneyhard-law.com/rev20041129.cfm.

——. *More Soft Money, Hard Law.* Washington, DC: Perkins Coie LLP, 2003.

——. "When the Pols Make the Calls: *McConnell's* Theory of Judicial Deference in the Twilight of Buckley." *University of Pennsylvania Law Review* 153 (2004): 5–30.

Bender, Paul. "The Canadian Charter of Rights and Freedoms and the United States Bill of Rights: A Comparison." *McGill Law Journal* 28 (1983): 811–66.

Bessette, Joseph. *The Mild Voice of Reason: Deliberative Democracy and American National Government.* Chicago: The University of Chicago Press, 1994.

Bickel, Alexander M. *The Least Dangerous Branch: The Supreme Court at the Bar of Politics.* Indianapolis: Bobbs–Merrill, 1962.

Bredt, Christopher D., and Markus F. Kremer. "Section 3 of the *Charter*: Democratic Rights at the Supreme Court of Canada." *National Journal of Constitutional Law* 17 (2005): 19–70.

Breyer, Stephen G. *Active Liberty: Interpreting Our Democratic Constitution.* New York: Alfred A. Knopf, 2005.

——. "Our Democratic Constitution." Harvard University Tanner Lectures (2004). Available at http://www.supremecourtus.gov/publicinfo/speeches/sp_11-17-04.html.

Cameron, Jamie. "Governance and Anarchy in the s. 2(b) Jurisprudence: A Comment on *Vancouver Sun* and *Harper v. Canada*." *National Journal of Constitutional Law* 17 (2005): 71–103.

Charlton, Mark, and Paul Barker, eds. *Crosscurrents: Contemporary Political Issues.* Scarborough, ON: Thompson/Nelson, 2002.

Christie, Les. "Kelo's Revenge: Voters Restrict Eminent Domain." 8 November 2006. Available at http://www.CNNMoney.com.

Courtney, John C. "The Franchise, Voter Registration and Electoral Districting: Who Says Canada is Just Like the United States?" Paper presented at the Annual Meeting of the American Political Science Association, Philadelphia, PA, August 2003.

Courtney, John C., Peter MacKinnon, and David E. Smith, eds. *Drawing Boundaries: Legislatures, Courts, and Electoral Values.* Saskatoon: Fifth House, 1992.

Daly, Elizabeth. "Idealists, Pragmatists and Textualists: Judging Electoral Districts in America, Canada and Australia." *Boston College International & Comparative Law Review* 21 (1998): 261–383.

Davidson, Chandler, and Bernard Grofman, eds. *Quiet Revolution in the South: The Impact of the Voting Rights Act, 1965–1990.* Princeton, NJ: Princeton University Press, 1994.

Days, Drew S. III. "Civil Rights in Canada: An American Perspective." *American Journal of Comparative Law* 32 (1984): 328–38.

Dworkin, Ronald. *Taking Rights Seriously.* Cambridge: Harvard University Press, 1977.

Ely, John Hart. *Democracy and Distrust.* Cambridge: Harvard University Press, 1980.

Ewing, K.D., and Samuel Issacharoff, eds. *Party Funding and Campaign Financing in International Perspective.* Oxford: Hart Publishing, 2006.

Feasby, Colin. "Issue Advocacy and Third Parties in the United Kingdom and Canada." *McGill Law Journal* 48 (2003): 11–54.

——. "*Libman v. Quebec (A.G.)* and the Administration of the Process of Democracy under the Charter: The Emerging Egalitarian Model." *McGill Law Journal* 44 (1999): 5–39.

Fiss, O. *The Irony of Free Speech.* Cambridge: Harvard University Press, 1996.

——. "Money and Politics." *Columbia Law Review* 97 (1997): 2470–83.

Franklin, Charles H., and Liane C. Kosaki. "Republican Schoolmaster: The U.S. Supreme Court, Public Opinion, and Abortion." *American Political Science Review* 83 (1989): 751–71.

Glendon, Mary Ann. *Rights Talk: The Impoverishment of Political Discourse.* New York: Free Press, 1991.

Gold, Alan D. "The Legal Rights Provisions—A New Vision or Déjà Vu." *Supreme Court Law Review* 4 (1982): 107–32.

Guinier, Lani. *The Tyranny of the Majority.* New York: The Free Press, 1994.

Hamilton, Alexander, James Madison, and John Jay. *The Federalist.* Edited by Clinton Rossiter. New York: Signet, 2003.

Hasen, Richard L. "The Political Market Metaphor and Election Law: A Comment on Issacharoff and Pildes." *Stanford Law Review* 50 (February 1998): 719–30.

Hennigar, Matthew. "Government Appeals as Dialogue: Expanding a Contemporary Debate." Paper presented at the Annual Meeting of the Canadian Political Science Association, Halifax, NS, May 2003.

Hiebert, Janet L. *Limiting Rights: The Dilemma of Judicial Review.* Montreal and Kingston: McGill–Queen's University Press, 1996.

Hogg, Peter W. "The Charter of Rights and American Theories of Interpretation." *Osgoode Hall Law Journal* 25 (1987): 87–113.

———. *Constitutional Law of Canada.* 2d ed. Toronto: Carswell, 1985.

———. *Constitutional Law of Canada.* 3d ed. Toronto: Carswell, 1992.

Hogg, Peter W., and Allison A. Bushell. "The Charter Dialogue between Courts and Legislatures." *Osgoode Hall Law Journal* 35 (1997): 75–107.

Hutchinson, Allan. *Waiting for Coraf: A Critique of Law and Rights.* Toronto: University of Toronto Press, 1995.

Issacharoff, Samuel. "Gerrymandering and Political Cartels." *Harvard Law Review* 116 (2002): 593–648.

Issacharoff, Samuel, and Richard Pildes. "Politics as Markets: Partisan Lockups of the Democratic Process." *Stanford Law Review* 50 (1998): 643-717.

Jenkins, Richard W. "Untangling the Politics of Electoral Boundaries in Canada, 1993–1997." *The American Review of Canadian Studies* 28 (1998): 517–38.

Karlan, Pamela. "The Rights to Vote: Some Pessimism about Formalism." *Texas Law Review* 71 (1993): 1705–40.

Katz, Richard S., and Peter Mair, eds. *How Parties Organize: Change and Adaptation in Party Organizations in Western Democracies.* London: Sage Publications, 1994.

Klarman, Michael. "The Puzzling Resistance to Political Process Theory." *Virginia Law Review* 77 (1991): 747–832.

Knopff, Rainer, and F.L. Morton. *Charter Politics.* Scarborough, ON: Nelson Canada, 1992.

Kurland, Philip, ed. *The Supreme Court Review.* Chicago: University of Chicago Press, 1967.

Kymlicka, Will, and Wayne Norman. "Return of the Citizen: A Survey of Recent Work on Citizenship Theory." *Ethics* 104 (1994): 360–69.

MacIvor, Heather. "The Charter of Rights and Party Politics: The Impact of the Supreme Court Ruling in *Figueroa v. Canada (Attorney General).*" Montreal: Institute for Research on Public Policy, *Choices* 10 (2004): 2–26.

Manfredi, Christopher. *Judicial Power and the Charter.* 2d ed. New York: Oxford University Press, 2001.

———. "Judicial Power and the *Charter*: Reflections on the Activism Debate." *UNB Law Journal* 53 (2004): 185–97.

McDonald, Michael P., and John Samples, eds. *The Marketplace of Democracy: Electoral Competition and American Politics.* Washington, DC: Brookings Institution Press, 2006.

McDowell, Gary, ed. *Taking the Constitution Seriously: Essays on the Constitution and Constitutional Law.* Dubuque, IA: Kendall/Hunt, 1981.

Monahan, Patrick. *Politics and the Constitution: The Charter, Federalism and the Supreme Court of Canada.* Toronto: Carswell, 1987.

Morton, F.L. "Canada's Judge Bork: Has the Counter–Revolution Begun?" *Constitutional Forum* 7 (1996): 121–25.

——. "The Politics of Rights: What Canadians Should Know About the American Bill of Rights." *Windsor Review of Legal and Social Issues* 1 (1989): 61–96.

Morton, F.L., and Rainer Knopff. *The Charter Revolution & the Court Party*. Peterborough, ON: Broadview Press, 2000.

Note. "The Disenfranchisement of Ex–Felons: Citizenship, Criminality, and the 'Purity of the Ballot Box.'" *Harvard Law Review* 102 (1989): 1300–17.

Peacock, Anthony, ed. *Rethinking the Constitution*. Toronto: Oxford University Press, 1996.

Persily, Nathaniel. "In Defense of Foxes Guarding Henhouses: The Case for Judicial Acquiescence to Incumbent–Protecting Gerrymanders." 116 *Harvard Law Review* (2002): 649–84.

Pitkin, Hanna. *The Concept of Representation*. Berkeley: University of California Press, 1967.

Polsby, Daniel D., and Robert D. Popper. "Ugly: An Inquiry into the Problem of Racial Gerrymandering under the Voting Rights Act." *Michigan Law Review* 92 (1993): 652–82.

Roach, Kent. "Dialogue or Defiance: Legislative Reversals of Supreme Court Decisions in Canada and the United States." *International Journal of Constitutional Law* 4 (2006): 347–70.

——. *The Supreme Court on Trial: Judicial Activism or Democratic Dialogue*. Toronto: Irwin Law, 2001.

Romanow, Roy, John Whyte, and Howard Leeson. *Canada Notwithstanding: The Making of the Constitution, 1976–1982*. Toronto: Carswell/Methuen, 1984.

Ryden, David K., ed. *The U.S. Supreme Court and the Electoral Process*. Washington, DC: Georgetown University Press, 2000.

Sancton, Andrew. "Eroding Representation by Population in the Canadian House of Commons: The *Representation Act*, 1985." *Canadian Journal of Political Science* 23 (1992): 441–57.

Schauer, Frederick. "Judicial Review of the Devices of Democracy." *Columbia Law Review* 94 (1994): 1326–47.

Scruton, Roger. *A Dictionary of Political Thought*. London: Pan Books, 1983.

Shapiro, Martin, and Alec Stone Sweet, eds. *On Law, Politics and Judicialization*. Oxford: Oxford University Press, 2002.

Smith, C. Lynn. "Adding a Third Dimension: The Canadian Approach to Constitutional Equality Guarantees." *Law and Contemporary Problems* 55 (1992): 211–34.

Stone, Dennis, and F. Kim Walpole. "The Canadian Constitution Act and the Constitution of the United States: A Comparative Analysis." *Canadian–American Law Journal* 2 (1983): 1–36.

Sunstein, C. *Democracy and the Problem of Free Speech*. Toronto: Maxwell Macmillan, 1993.

Tarnopolsky, Walter S. "The New Canadian Charter of Rights and Freedoms as Compared and Contrasted with the American Bill of Rights." *Human Rights Quarterly* 5 (1983): 227–74.

Tocqueville, Alexis de. *Democracy in America*. 1835. Translated by Francis Bowen. 1862. New York: Vintage Books, 1945.

Tribe, Laurence. *American Constitutional Law*. Mineola, NY: Foundation Press, 1978.

——. "The Puzzling Persistence of Process–Based Constitutional Theories." *Yale Law Journal* 89 (1979–80): 1063–80.

Tushnet, Mark. "Policy Distortion and Democratic Debilitation: Comparative Illumination of the Countermajoritarian Difficulty." *Michigan Law Review* 94 (1995): 245–301.

Valelley, Richard, ed. *The Voting Rights Act: Securing the Ballot*. Washington, DC: Congressional Quarterly Press, 2006.

Williams, Russell Alan. "The 279 Formula: and Federal Redistributions: Canada's System of Representation in Crisis." *Annual Review of Canadian Studies* 35 (2005): 99–134.

——. "Comparing Federal Electoral Redistributions: Straining Canada's System of Representation." Paper presented at the Annual Meeting of the Canadian Political Science Association, Quebec City, QC, June 2001.

Index